3 PEAS
IN THE
70s

Dedication

To two lovely old gentlemen, both of whom were great encouragers in the publication of *3 Peas in a Pram*. Sadly missed.

Alan Henry Butler died 19.3.2021
Paul Stephenson died 29.9.2020

Introduction

I began writing Book two at the start of the Covid pandemic in December 2019. The United Kingdom's government placed us in lockdown for the first time in March 2020. The weeks and months passed, making it clearer that we wouldn't be continuing life as normal in the near future. Restrictions, rules and social distancing were put in place to reduce the spread of the virus. These were:

- Remaining socially distant at all times, being two metres apart.
- Remaining vigilant and always obeying the latest guidelines.

This has caused people in the world to be gripped by fear, anxiety and uncertainty about the future. It's caused panic buying of toilet rolls and flour. Yet amid these cataclysmic changes, there have been many random acts of kindness to complete strangers, as well as hundreds of food banks springing up to feed those in need.

As I have travelled through lockdown, not seeing family caused health problems to rise up in me. Why should this be a surprise, as issues in my past required attention? It made sense, with the world in such turmoil, due to the Covid virus. In addition to that, the total number of deaths were being flashed up from every country on the television daily. Past bereavements began to surface, along with the fear of death and the dentist, causing me to travel on the road of forgiveness yet again.

During this time, the value of family, friends and neighbours, has been highlighted, causing me to realise the importance of other human beings. Pastimes like clothes shopping and eating out have fallen by the way side. Thank Heaven for the beautiful months of sunshine during the summertime, allowing us to spend time in our gardens and go on a walk.

With thousands of deaths linked to this virus, many of these people will have died without loved ones by their side. Yet again, the kindness of the National Health Service staff filled this gap, bringing comfort, help and healing to so many needy folks.

I know people have disagreed with some measures and steps the government have taken along this unprecedented journey to put Great Britain back on its feet again, but I trust and pray for wisdom for these people in leadership to make correct decisions. Only time will tell how this pandemic will play out – the lives lost, the people healed and how society will evolve in dealing with future outbreaks.

One of the joys in taking my short daily walks was smelling the wild roses in gardens and hedgerows along the way. This fragrance took me straight back to my childhood, collecting petals to make perfume. Us girls would go to Albert Park in Middlesbrough to the rose garden, stuffing petals that had fallen to the ground into our pockets. The official title for this place was *Garden of Fragrance*. It was commissioned in September 1955 for the Golden Jubilee of the Rotary Club. The original plan and cost would total £461 with labels in braille. Eventually, a payment was agreed of £376 to include a plaque with the Rotary Club's name and involvement on it. Arriving home with our bounty, we would ask Mam for a jam jar and add water to the petals. Leaving these to soak overnight, we got up the following morning to dab on our finished perfume. Perfect.

Original envelope from Buckingham Palace containing a gift of £3 to our mother after our birth

3 Peas in a Pram

Tying Up Loose Ends

I would like to begin from a place of thanksgiving. After completing a book signing session on 25.2.2017, a dark-haired lady approached me asking if I was Leo Harcourt's granddaughter. The question surprised me. She explained that her sister, Joyce, and her husband Joe Harland had rented rooms at 7 Windsor Road, in Linthorpe Village – Grandad Leo's address.

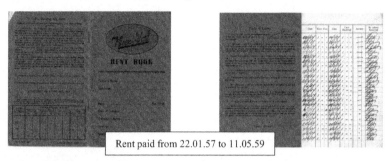

Rent paid from 22.01.57 to 11.05.59

I met up with this lovely couple, and the first thing Joyce showed me was her old rent book from sixty years ago. I had written out a list of questions, and slowly having them answered, I began to have a glimpse of a long-lost grandad and part of our family history.

Outside 7 Windsor Road with Aunty Katy, Gillian, Rosemary and Frances – 13th July 1961

Grandad Leo had a strong Catholic faith and had a wooden cross on the wall in the kitchen. He was very kind and caring. She remembers Leo taking care of her and phoning for an ambulance when she had her son, Andrew. Her labour started in the middle of the night, and as her husband was at work, Leo ran around to the phone box. They had Sunday dinners together, sharing the cost of the meat from the March butchers in Skelton. Every other Sunday tea was spent with Uncle Alan and his family visiting – both families sat in the kitchen together. Then in the evening, Grandad went to church to the Holy Name of Mary.

One day there was a knock on the door, and Joyce could hear Leo talking to his neighbour, Mrs Branigan. As he came back into the room, his first words were, "Well, Rene's been found". He always spoke in a matter-of-fact way, and this was his quiet reaction to his only daughter's whereabouts. He then proceeded to tell Joyce where she was living, along with the fact she had given birth to triplets.

On returning from his search for his family in Coventry, Leo spent hours making three low pink chairs in the kitchen extension. He shared with Joyce that he was pleased with how Mam was managing with us all, even though he couldn't understand her leaving the water running whilst rinsing our clothes.

A postcard has come to light dated 10.8.1960 on which is written, "Leo is still at Rene's (Mam's), they have tonsillitis, and he is looking after them". It was music to my ears to know that Grandad often visited us. Joyce confirmed this was the case and recalls he visited Coventry often.

Owing to Grandad's military career, he was very capable and conscientious, having a personality trait of being orderly and a desire to do a task well. When we turned up on his doorstep on 13.7.1961, with nowhere to live, Leo had no hesitation in agreeing with the decision for us triplets to be placed in the children's home, Nazareth House. He was happy for us to go, believing we would be in safe hands and cared for by a religious body.

Picture of Joe, Leo, Rene, Joyce and Celia – Oct/Nov 1958

Prior to this drama, Joyce and Joe had moved house to a council estate at Easterside, although Joe stated he didn't want to leave 7 Windsor Road. Grandad Leo continued to rent his property and took in other lodgers from a local coal merchant called Woodhouse. Two weeks after we were placed in care, this property was sold.

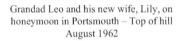

Grandad Leo and his new wife, Lily, on honeymoon in Portsmouth – Top of hill August 1962

There was a golden window of opportunity for Grandad Leo and Mam to be reconciled with one another. Although her father was a man of principle, having morally correct behaviour, he was lonely, so it must have delighted him to have his only child back under his roof.

I can only imagine that those ten days would have been filled with him treating his thirty-year-old daughter with kindness.

He was rightly concerned with practical matters and must have been very grateful to his nephew, Alan, for his kind offer of allowing Mam and Ann into his already busy household after the sale of 7 Windsor Road. Knowing it would bless his family in the future, he helped Mam select furniture that he no longer needed from his four bedroomed property that would be stored in the dining room in his nephew's home. Whatever happened, they had a lot to catch up on before Grandad's marriage to Lily.

With so much upheaval in such a short space of time, Mam won't have known if she was at the park or the pictures. However, the weight of responsibility for her three daughters' care was temporarily lifted for now. She had carried this daily care for four years – not an easy task – with only Dad having any supporting role to speak of.

Now separated from her husband and her three daughters in care, the only role she had left to play was to support her youngest daughter, Ann. However, the thread of reconciliation would later be woven into our parents' lives when they got back together, making way for a reunion with Ann and her three sisters on the 7th of July 1962.

I had the thought that Dad must have been really proud when he eventually kept his promise and collected the three of us from Nazareth House, taking us home to 5 Mary Ann Street. I haven't

given Mam much credit for our return home, nor Grandad Leo either.

In hindsight, though, each person had their own part to play – Grandad hearing about the sale of 5 Mary Ann

Ann aged two years

Street, and then Mam asking Grandad Leo for the deposit money. It's strange, but none of us actually remember returning to our parents, but hopefully, we no longer felt unwanted. I think this was especially important to Gilly as she remembers Dad promising to come back for us.

Mum with her arms full – Reunited at three months old

Chapter One – Words

The words, "Snap, Crackle, Pop", "Matchstick legs," and "Specky four eyes" continued to be spoken over us throughout our secondary education. With the boys at St Thomas' Roman Catholic School in Middlesbrough, adding to our vocabulary any words with a three-letter connotation or implications that are too rude to repeat.

An exception to this was a lad called Shaun – he used to burst into song every time he saw me, giving a lovely rendition of Don Partridge's song called *Rosie*. These lyrics were an antidote to the harsh bullying inflicted by other kids.

The words sang over me were:

> *Rosie, oh Rosie*
> *I'd paint your face for all the world to see.*
> *Rosie, oh Rosie*
> *I'd like to paint your face eternally.*

Even now, this song brings a smile to my face.

St Thomas' school photos of Rosemary (Left) and Gillian (Right) 1969

We kept mainly to ourselves during school time, meeting up with each other on a lunch break, as the number three was never a crowd in our case. Settling into secondary education, we were encouraged by our parents to have a high set of morals and a good work ethic. We were seen as model pupils, and we were all in top sets in our individual classes.

Occasionally, fights broke out between different schools in the area, with rival pupils arranging to meet at the *White Bridge*, notorious for such confrontations. Pupils would remove their ties in preparation and stream out of the school gates. Us three would remain at our desks, scared and frightened of what would take place as the young people would stand their ground to fight. I remember St Thomas' School was quiet. The teachers and staff would have been needed to quell the violent behaviour between the teenagers looking for trouble at the end of term.

We were three quiet, unassuming girls in public, but being triplets, we stood out in a crowd. This occasionally worked in our favour. Even at the teenage age of thirteen, we would go and watch the Middlesbrough footballers practise on the fields at Hutton Road, not far from school. We became friends with some of the younger players, who would sometimes walk us home and come in for a soft drink. Dad had his hands full as some became boyfriend material, but eventually, these budding relationships fizzled out when the lads found out we were *good girls*. Maybe these events set in motion our Dad arranging a meeting with the head, Mr Bryan. Both our parents were in full agreement for the three of us to continue our secondary education at St Mary's Convent School, as we had all achieved impressive 2nd, 3rd and 5th places within our year groups.

1st year convent photos of Rosemary (Left) and Gillian (Right) 1971. Unfortunately, the school photos of Frances are missing.

The headmaster was in favour of us remaining where we were as this would improve *their* achievement record. In hindsight, it was one of our parents' best decisions. Giving me a love of reading and writing, culminating in the long process of producing my own book, *3 Peas in a Pram*.

So, the decision had been made, we were to enrol at St Mary's Convent in Saltersgill Avenue, Middlesbrough, Yorkshire, to begin the next stage of our education from September 1970.

St Mary's Convent was run by the Faithful Companions of Jesus. Way back in 1872, Bishop Cornthwaite invited M. Josephine Petit (Second General Supervisor) to make a foundation, with special hope working among the destitute girls and women. He laid great importance on schools and evening classes. In 1885 the nuns moved to a site on Newlands Road in Middlesbrough called The Newlands. This community moved again to Saltersgill Avenue in 1963 to a brand-new school building. The Catholic Sisters made three vows:

1)   Poverty: the freedom to give. We share all things in common, recognising the human and ecological impact of the drive for ownership and possession.
2)   Chastity: the freedom to love. Offering our whole heart to God through this vow, we seek to love all people.
3)   Obedience: the freedom to live. This vow calls us to attentive listening to God's will, inviting others into our lives and decisions.
See the website fcjsisters.org

These vows were an earnest promise of this religious order to behave and act in love and assurance of help when needed. The three of us were to learn the hard way, emotionally, that these Christian women didn't always practise what they preached. Words were spoken over us, a kind of *do as I say, not as I do*, fuelling mistaken ideas about who God is.

During the six-week summer holiday in 1970, we kept in touch with Julie, Bernie and Pat. Julie said it was hard being friends of triplets, but it worked as they were friends with one of us at a time. Around this time, we asked our mam if we could buy some new underwear, recalling to mind the fact that I found out about periods from the lollipop lady. Of course, Mam had no input into how we should navigate this sensitive topic but thrust money into our hands to go shopping for a bra. Thankfully, our slightly older friend, Bernie, knew exactly where to go shopping for such items. We all had exactly the same shaped figures as triplets, and one size would fit us all. With help and guidance from the shop assistant, we all fell out of the shop giggling with embarrassment, happily clutching brown bags with our new accessories to cover our figures from unwanted attention. This lovely friend also asked permission from Mam to buy us makeup for our birthdays.

Sadly, Bernice had dyslexia and had to stay on at St Thomas' School, but she occasionally remembers walking over to the convent and meeting up with us all. Julie also remained there, and only Pat followed us to the convent. Sometimes we fell out with these girlfriends but never with each other, continuing to be happy with each other's company.

The beginning of September 1970 heralded changes that would shape the next five years in our young lives. I remember feeling physically sick in the lead-up to this new term. After taking out money for our uniforms for St Thomas' School, our parents had to find extra funds to buy the three of us the brand-new uniforms required. No doubt applying for a school grant from the local council. Back in the 1970s, Newlands uniforms could be purchased at several shops in Middlesbrough – Ross's, Baums and New Houses costing around seven pounds. Maybe Mam had put a late application in for school clothing, or perhaps the shops had run out of certain sizes (remember she needed three of everything). Whatever the reason, we started our first day, still wearing part of our old uniform. Maybe this was a reminder of our social disadvantage to the nuns, causing Sister Bernadette to have my sisters and I stand up in assembly for not wearing the correct uniform. This headmistress knew of our family's circumstances and showed little compassion as we all blushed with shame. I quickly learned to despise her for causing us such a feeling of humiliation, viewed by our peers and staff.

I have come across a quote from those times, stating, "Uniform is the first line of defence for the more important rules to follow, maintaining balance and order within the school setting". Maybe this is one of the reasons Sister Bernadette would harp on about pupils not in full uniform, wanting to bring equality at the start of a new term. You would have thought common sense would have prevailed, as it was no fault of our own that money was tight. Our parents had other bills to pay and four hungry mouths to feed.

This all-girls school focused on teaching the Catholic faith, and rules and regulations were to be obeyed for a fruitful school life. This was a hard transformation coming from a disadvantaged background, with the three of us finding it extremely hard to find our feet, being taught alongside intelligent girls from well to do areas around Teesside. We quickly found ourselves dropping like stones to the bottom of the barrel. It would take two years for us to become familiar and grow in confidence in this new regime. Each day began with assembly, consisting of Catholic hymns and prayers, maybe including a line of, "Thank you, Lord, for the gift of learning and the gift of Catholic education". Our school week consisted of us walking to and from the convent four times a day; due to the fact we didn't stop for school dinners. Up and down Hereford Close, Lancaster Road, The Avenue, Emerson Avenue and then onto Saltersgill Avenue – nearly two miles each way, making us *as fit as fleas*. I now know, in hindsight, this was a good thing as we were well fed at home. One girl shared with me that she was unhappy at the convent and always hungry in her first year there. This was because the first-year girls would be last in the queue for lunch.

Often there was no food left as it had all been given out. She remembers a teacher going to speak to the kitchen staff and them being asked to make small doughnuts covered in sugar. No point in telling your parents. Her parents could afford for her to travel to school on the bus, where the young people were segregated – the boys went on the top deck, and the girls sat downstairs, telling jokes on the backseats.

Advice from the nuns was for young ladies not to wear patent leather shoes, as the boys could see up their skirts in the reflection.

This initial year carried some challenging experiences for our parents too. Mam was invited to watch a video on sex education within the school setting along with other parents before us pupils were allowed to see it. She was highly embarrassed. Returning home that evening, clutching a brown envelope, Mam said it was a book for us to read, but it had to be kept under a pillow as Ann, our younger sister, was not allowed to look at it. Even after watching the video at school, boys were still aliens, and the everyday workings of their bodies were still a mystery to us naïve girls. Sometimes our Ann would ask awkward questions, with Dad passing the baton to us. Gilly recalls her younger sister asking her, not Mam, about periods as it was too embarrassing. Our parents were both very private. They eventually gave permission for Ann to look through the black and white book on sex education, no doubt leaving her as baffled as we were. Our education on the birds and the bees would have been much clearer if we had had a brother.

On returning home at the end of a school day, we had a snack and a drink. Then under our parents' watchful eye, we sat around the table to do homework with Mam helping if we got stuck. She had already prepared the tea which was cooking in the oven, and each evening wafted around the house as we waited for Dad to get home from work to eat it. Although we were poor, we ate traditional food of meat and vegetables, with the best steak being reserved for the man of the house.

It was very rare for two of us to be poorly and absent from school at the same time, but I remember feeling very lonely walking to school on my tod. Gilly once had tonsillitis and bronchitis, with Mam putting her in the boxroom, and Ann had to sleep in with us. I remember Mam's care increased when one of us fell ill, giving us treats of tomato soup and special puddings to tempt us to eat.

Growing up, we were under the illusion that all nuns and the priesthood had taken this worthy vocation because they had been called by God. This made it difficult to envisage a good or loving God because of some of their negative behaviour towards us. A wiser person explained that this was not necessarily so. Catholics had large families, and tradition at that time was for a child to enter into this vocation as a means to have them fed, watered and educated. It was also considered very prestigious to have an Irish daughter become a Nun, as having a son in the Priesthood. Sometimes this was thrust upon them and not of their own choice, maybe causing surprising responses to life's experiences among laypeople.

After a lovely sunny weekend, it was time for Sister Bernadette to receive a taste of her own medicine. The whole school filed into assembly on the Monday morning, with us triplets spying on our cousins, Janet and Deborah, as we sat down on the hall floor with them. As we lifted our heads, we could see that our headmistress had been in the sun. She explained that she had fallen asleep and woken up to find one half of her face bright red, with the other cheek white. Well, some of the girls started to snigger and soon the whole hall filled with laughter – I joined in but did feel sorry for her, though.

In later years, we were treated more kindly, especially by Sister Marie Teresa, who taught religious education. She was a sweet young nun, wedded to God, who lived her Christian faith within the classroom. She was an effective teacher, showing her pupils how to set out their lessons, giving clear examples of what was expected of us with various projects. This lady was very kind, and we were sad to hear that she had left the order after the A-Level exams had been taken. Our young tongues were wagging after a rumour started making the rounds that she had run away with a priest. The true reason never surfaced.

The year of our O-Levels brought to light the fact our English teacher gave us the wrong book to read for the syllabus. One of our joys in life was reading; with Mam helping us with our revision, I was really confident that my hard work would pay off. The exam was a disaster as no one could answer one of the questions, and the whole of the year had to re-sit it the following year.

In our art exam, the three of us chose to draw still life – wood and mice, I think. Our artwork was often put on display in the main corridor. However, the person marking the papers thought we had cheated, not realising we were triplet sisters. So, we failed O-Level art as well. No wonder we hated sitting exams. Some memories would be better erased from our brains forever. Not so with the three of us volunteering with Cross Link. This was an international Mission Society with its roots in the Bible.

Another of life's experiences was when our lovely art teacher, Mrs Tinkler, asked our parents' permission for the three of us to visit her house out of school hours. I can't remember the precise reason for this adventure, but it found us feeding her goats and looking at the beehive. She lived in Nunthorpe on Gypsy Lane, and we had to climb up to her home. Looking around, I thought this was a place I would like to live when I was married. Now I do.

Part of our 'worship' included shopping for an old couple called Mr and Mrs Devonport. They lived in a street house in the town, and we took turns doing their weekly food shopping. Mr D was blind, so his wife was his *eyes*. In the years that followed, we grew to love them both, almost like grandparents. Sadly,

Mrs D became poorly and died, so we had to help her husband clear out their property as sheltered housing had been found for him on Marton Road in Middlesbrough. To our surprise, we discovered money (mainly in handbags), and when we told Mr D, he felt the banknotes and knew exactly what note was what. This hoard totalled thousands of pounds, and Gilly persuaded him it was time to open a bank account. Eventually, both Gilly and Francy left home, and I was the only one shopping for him. Sadly, one day after shopping for him and handing over his change, we had a fallout, and I was very upset. I wish I could have dealt with this event in a more grown-up fashion, just laughing it off, but I stopped visiting.

Years later, he had a fall and broke his hip, eventually dying of pneumonia. Thankfully, he didn't have a pauper's funeral, as Gilly got in touch with the coroner, advising him that Mr D's cleaner had his bank and building society books. Only seven people attended his funeral. We were told he had kept asking for us to visit him in hospital, but we never knew. Such a sad ending to this story, but hopefully, we brought a lot of love and joy into his life, helping to navigate life's storms, as he had no children of his own.

Photos of Mr and Mrs Davenport dated 1916

Death is such a hard word, along with hospital, cancer and suffering. So often, communicating a scary image, disturbing one's peace of mind, making you feel unhappy, frightened, unsettled and worried. This becomes the focus of our lives, becoming a habit, often causing our imaginations to run away with us.

I have listed below some answers to a questionnaire on illness and death in the 1970s:

Anthony replied, *"Thankfully, it didn't happen very much whilst we were children. Mum's dad died in 1966 – I was aware of deep anguish and unhappiness – but we didn't go to his funeral or wake. Aunty Eleanor's was the first dead body I had seen. This was a dreadful shock, but apparently the Catholic way. That would have been in about 1970/71."*

My friend, Kim, wrote, *"My Nana was always unwell. She was very ill as a child and always had breathing problems with recurrent bronchitis, so we grew accustomed to seeing her as an invalid. My mother did a lot to help her. When I was 25, my 21-year-old cousin was killed in a car accident. I was in Hampshire, so I wasn't around, but all the aunts, uncles and cousins rallied around to support his family. The same happened when another cousin committed suicide. When my mam's mother/siblings have died, everyone has talked openly about it and supported each other...even to the extent of singing/praying at the bedside during the final hours."*

Joan, an older lady, wrote, *"There has been much loss and illness in the family. There is only one instance where I wish I could go back in time when my husband died suddenly at the age of 41. Our children were 7 and 4 years old. My mother said the children were too young to go to his funeral (my father was already dead by this time). Most other family members felt the same way and were in no state to know what would be best. Since then, things have changed, and children are no longer 'shielded' from grief but allowed to express themselves more openly. I think adults are too. I remember keeping a stiff upper lip for the sake of the children but looking back, I think it was a mistake. It was the way of things then, though."*

Anne Dennis replied, *"My dad died in 1966 (the World Cup year), so my mum was very protective of my sisters and I. But I guess Mum was only worried we would be hurt in some way. Then my grandfather came to live with us, but he died in 1970. Then my grandma died, all before the age of eleven – having a profound effect on my life. Missed not having a dad – hated Father's Day and having no dad to pick me up from the dance etc."*

My sister-in-law, Helen, stated, *"There were a couple of deaths in our family (Aunty Florrie, Uncle Bob). It was not really talked about, and as a child, I was certainly not allowed to go to the funeral. Worse still was when Aunty Alice died the night before your wedding. Not sure how we kept it together that day! Mam had a hysterectomy when I was about 8 and was in the hospital for about 10 days. Aunty Alice stayed with us to 'run the house', and I was told Mam had a bad leg!"*

The Cross

Have you looked towards that sign?
A sign of the Father's love
For you and me?
Not how you think or imagine
But how it was to be

Have you looked towards that sign?
A sign of the Father's love
For you and me?
Not how you think or imagine
But how it was to be

His blood was shed in history
from past to present to Eternity
Christ chose to die upon that tree
Once and for all for you and me

His friendship and His love for you
Crossed the bridge of death and sin
To raise you up in resurrection.
Thank Him for the cost
Of His hurt and pain
To bring you back to God again

The choice is yours
Will you come by GRACE?
Kneel and accept this love
From Jesus Christ in heaven above?

And then join in glorious song
Giving thanks all day long
For he has risen this Easter day
To enable us to follow THE WAY!

My own personal experience of loss was back in 1968. Grandad Leo had died of cancer, and I remember feeling sad for Mam. I cried myself to sleep for months, thinking that everyone I loved in my family would die, whereas it was not until we were in our fifties that both our parents passed away. Such worry would have been needless if a responsible adult had made the choice of words in explaining that this was the natural process of life. As a child, the only sermon I remember was by Father Crowley – that hell and damnation awaited you if you decorated the house on a Sunday. We returned home to find Mam wallpapering the front room. Gilly recalls being frightened that Mam would go to hell for this and was only reassured this would not be so after talking to Sister Marie Teresa during her A-Levels. Clearly, our imaginations can change our perceptions of reality, causing mental distress from a concern of something impending or anticipated in our lives. This is unhealthy and may cause mental health issues resulting from life's hard knocks. Last Easter, I pondered the subject of death, and a poem rose up within me. I have included it here.

Let me tell you, there is no one beyond God's grace and ability to save and make new. The Bible states this truth as follows,

For God is one, and there is one mediator between God and the sons of man – the true man, Jesus, The Anointed One. He gave himself as the ransom   payment for <u>everyone</u>."

You can hold God at his _word_.

I have put together a list of support organisations in the appendix at the back of this book to help support you, as the reader, in becoming reconciled to your past life experiences.

Clearly, Mam's ill-health stemmed from her husband working abroad in Saudi. She wrote to my father stating:

"You are always in my thoughts, and I worry about you every day."

Around January 1976, it became apparent that Mam was feeling depressed. Her thoughts and imagination had indeed become a habit, with worry becoming the focus in her everyday life. This carried on for months. Then in April 1976 (after Dad had been home on holiday), he returned to find out he was being moved to Abqaiq, a Saudi Aramco gated community at the Estate's Province of Saudi Arabia. He too was suffering ill-health and had a _poorly tummy_. Mam clearly thought this was bad news, writing to him of her true feelings:

"I feel rather lost and depressed at the moment. It was very hard watching you going away in the taxi. I didn't want you to go back. Everyone was just getting used to you again and becoming a family unit again. I think the girls have changed since they started work. I don't feel as close to them as I used to, in fact I feel completely on my own most of the time."

I distinctly recall hearing Mam crying in the night but realised I could not prevent her pain. I must have shared this information with my sisters.
To alleviate some of life's burdens, we did our own washing, helped with housework and often cooked Sunday dinner. However, we were either at work or treating home as a hotel for the rest of the time. Maybe Mrs Greenheld encouraged our mother to make an appointment to see the doctor, as she wrote to Dad saying:

"I went down this morning for my blood test and had to wait ¾ of an hour in the waiting room, which was most annoying. The result should be back in a week. Take care of yourself and don't worry too much, I'm sure I will feel better soon. I miss you very much already, and don't forget I love you and think of you every day."

Dad, unknowingly, added to Mam's stress by not writing to let her know he had arrived safely to his destination:

"I have been very worried as there is still no letter from you. I keep telling myself that I would have heard from someone if there was anything wrong, and that probably they have sent you into the middle of the desert to do a special job. The last few nights, I have lain awake worrying and I can't seem to settle or put my mind to anything."

The following week after Easter, Mam put pen to paper yet again, writing:

"At long last, two welcome letters from you arrived on Saturday. A red-letter day for me! So pleased to hear you arrived safely and had a good journey."

Although there is no mention of our mam taking anti-depressants, she was given little brown tablets to take by her doctor. Then, recording the results of other blood tests, she informs Dad:

"The doctor said the result of this blood test was excellent. There was no sign of anaemia at all, and he was really pleased with it. He asked if I thought the tablets were helping me, and I said I was coping better but still felt depressed. So now I have a month's supply of the same tablets."

21

I also wrote to Dad on the 7th of June 1976, letting him know:

Mum is feeling better, I can tell because she doesn't shout as much now. She's getting very proud of the garden and often waters the plants."

Dad had at last begun to write more often, with Mam recording her happiness, writing:

"Many thanks for your lovely letters. I can't tell you how much they mean to me. I treasure every word you write, and they cheer me up when I am down."

There appear to be no more airmail letters written to Dad after the 16th of June 1976. Thankfully for Mam, he returned home on the 3rd of July 1976 and spent the following six months unemployed until beginning employment with IFS Electrical Contractors as a Foreman Electrician in the following December.

After reading a recording in print, in such personal words from Mam to Dad, I think that her husband was clearly her everything then. She didn't have many close friends (only Mrs Greenheld). She no longer visited Aunty Celia, nor did her previous best friend visit her. There may have been a rift or fallout somewhere along that line. My cousin Anthony certainly thinks that it was odd. Whatever was wrong, Mam never talked about it to her daughters, maybe wanting to protect us about how she was. I clearly remember her having difficulty concentrating, feeling tired and fatigued. I felt frustrated that it seemed to take forever for her to cook and prepare Sunday teas. Taking tablets also contributed to her falling asleep early evening and then sleeping all night.

Sometimes growing up, I would wonder if I actually knew her at all. Mam certainly put on a brave face when mixing with relatives, with people thinking she was a happy person. My mother may have had a unique reason to feel *the tired thoughts of a tired mind*, especially raising four children under the age of two in the late 1950s. If only she could have received help and support available through counselling back then. It didn't help when Dad told her to pull herself together on more than one occasion. Obviously, he had little or no understanding of what it was like to feel as Mam did. A talking cure would have given my mother the much-needed understanding and non-judgemental help to unlock her particular cause of depression. Helping her think it through and help her move on. Our mam's generation was fearsomely impressive. She was born with an exceptional intellect that had her reading and memorising the dictionary as a child. A good counsellor may have been the keystone of her coming out of depression and living a life of well-being.

I personally felt very protective over our mam, especially when Dad was working abroad. Both Francy and I always bought her presents because we sensed she was unhappy and thought she needed cheering up. These airmail letters have been hidden gems, kept for such a time as this, recording Mam's appreciation of these small loving gestures of affection from all her daughters.

In December 1975, she wrote:

"Every time Rosie gets her money, she brings me a little present for the house. Now we have three kitchen knives and half a kitchen toolset. I've come to the opinion that I am getting spoilt."
"Rosie arrived back early saying the shops in Newcastle were great, so she bought me a beautiful picture. It is really a copper engraving of Alnwick and looks really expensive. Wasn't that nice of her?"
"Gill bought me some daffodils for Valentine's Day, so we had about four or five vases of flowers around the house."

In March 1976, Mam wrote to Dad letting him know:

"I had another lovely surprise on Saturday. Gill bought me some gorgeous flowers and Rosie and Frannie had one of their shopping sprees and came back with a really beautiful picture for me. It is an etching of Bambrough Castle in stainless steel, mounted on green hessian with a wooden frame. We had hung it over the fireplace, and everyone has been admiring it."

In April, she wrote:

"Frances bought some beautiful flowers for me. They look like double narcissus and also some freesias. The perfume from them fills the whole room."

It gives me comfort that our love and support spills out of these precious letters, and no doubt it would have blessed Dad to have these ordinary everyday accounts of his family's life back home.

Chapter Two – Worry

This may seem an unusual heading, but as children and adults, we have very different ways of coping when feeling anxious or distressed.

At thirteen years of age (1970), I remember walking my friend Julie home, as she had stopped at ours for tea. This will have been a weekend as it was late evening. We both nattered as we walked past Albert Park, the fire station, and then down the side of Clairville Common. As we neared Nazareth House, I noticed someone sitting on a bike watching us, and I warned Julie to be careful. I began to retrace my steps back home, but suddenly I heard a swish of bike wheels behind me. As I turned, I knew it was that man, and out of his mouth came a torrent of evil words that my thirteen-year-old ears had never heard before. My heart began to beat faster, and I took off running. I knew I was in danger and ran like the wind. Fear propelled me. Up ahead, I could see another figure walking towards me in the dark – another man. I felt frightened to say I was being followed, and by this time, I was near the houses past the fire station and felt safer. However, after a few minutes, I heard his voice again. The houses looked dark, and it never crossed my mind to knock on a door, so I just set off running once more. Suddenly, I fell, but I was quickly on my feet again. The fall had bruised my knees and put a hole in my new white loons, but by now, I was really close to Hereford Close, where I lived. Realising he hadn't followed me down the cut, I could finally feel my heart slowing down. Sweating and with butterflies in my tummy, I started to wonder how to mend the big rip in my loons. Falling in the back door, tea was ready, and it was my favourite – sausage and mash. For some reason, I didn't tell my parents about what had just happened, maybe thinking it was my fault.

Around the same period, I decided to walk to our local library on Marton Road. As kids, we walked everywhere. No wonder we had matchstick legs. I set out by myself, in the sunshine. As I walked towards Marton Road, the clouds appeared, and suddenly there was a peal of thunder. My books needed to be returned to the library to stop me from getting a fine, so I pressed on. Fear began to take hold as the storm increased with lightning strikes around me. As I hurried up the library steps, the storm was overhead. Thankfully, it had passed by the time I had handed my books and chosen the new ones to take back with me. No wonder Dad always wanted us to have another sister in tow. Boy, was I happy to get back home.

Living on our council estate was a mix of different families from all walks of life. I became friends with an older girl further up the road. According to my sisters, she was a bad influence, and I was soon swearing like a trooper. One afternoon there was a knock at the door, and I was asked if I wanted to go and see the tent in her family's back garden. So off we went. Opening the flap of the tent, I saw a lad was already in it. I sat down beside him, and my friend followed behind me. I had only been there a few minutes, and I could hear a male voice shouting, "Rosie!". Dad had found out where I had gone and wanted me home. Another lucky escape. From then on, I was banned from her house. Our parents were aware of dangers even if we weren't.

I often got myself into mischief of my own making, scrumping in a neighbour's garden on the opposite side of our road. Scrumping is an old-fashioned word for stealing apples either from a tree, orchard or store. In my defence, we were often hungry as kids, and I probably thought any apples on the ground would be wasted. As I came out of their gate, the family's dalmatian dog ran at me and bit me. As I was caught in the act, my parents had little sympathy for me.

These three memories would follow me into adulthood, surfacing in 2011, when I would need counselling to overcome the fear of dogs and walking alone on the hills near home.

Our young lives were spent worrying about pleasing our mother and father. Was this tied to a fear of being sent back to the children's home? We thought Dad had special powers as he would always catch us out doing something wrong. But, in reality, people would just casually mention they had seen us, one time on a bus, and Dad would ask what we had been up to.

Dad had a right to be concerned. I was meeting up out of school with a young lad called Gerald. By now, I was fourteen years old. He was a bit older or appeared to be, as he had a bike to get him to and from one of the council estates on the outskirts of Middlesbrough. I was naïve. Francy and I had gotten the bus to his house to meet his family – safety in numbers. Sitting in their front room was similar to our house. We were introduced to his mam and an older sister. Gerald must have asked me up to his bedroom, but closely followed on our heels was his mam.

Parents needed to be vigilant, and he was sent packing downstairs again whilst I used the bathroom. Francy and I must have had a good giggle about that on the bus back to town. Our friendship continued to blossom, and I bravely arranged to meet up with him during lunchtime. All went well until I was stopped coming back into the school building. Needless to say, it was the one and only time that it happened. My parents were immediately informed of my behaviour. I was told I was to stop seeing this young man. I was to ask him to our house one last time to tell him that my parents wanted us to break up. It broke my heart to see him crying at the news. It was the first time I had seen a lad crying. However, he continued to walk us triplets home after school but would peddle off before getting to the top of our road. One day, our dad leapt from around the corner and was really mad to find out that we were still seeing each other behind his back. It frightened the life out of us. My telling off continued down our road, with Mam joining in as we entered our house. Later that evening, something recoiled in me the horror of being treated that way, and I found myself running out of the house.

Dad ran after me but couldn't catch me as he was wearing his slippers, and soon got left behind. The only place I could think to run to was Sacred Heart Church, where I would feel safe. Evening mass was on, and I immediately recognised one of the helpers from our youth club. I sat quietly at the back of the church until mass had finished, and then this kind man asked me if I was ok. I burst into tears, telling him how unfair my parents were to stop me from seeing my boyfriend. He explained that my family would be worried about me. He stated that he would come back and explain where I had been and speak to them for me. On arriving home, I was told to go straight to my bedroom. I could hear them talking in hushed voices and whatever was said seemed to make the situation calmer, and I went to sleep. I had to stop seeing Gerald and was sad to see him with a new girlfriend a few months later.

Gillian in garden of Hereford Close 1977

Ann & Frances Hereford Close 1977

Looking back to this time in our teenage years, the three of us remember being unsettled. Especially struggling to catch up and cope with the exceptional education provided by the nuns in our new convent school. Gilly recalls it took her two years to settle and begin to grow in confidence and ability. In addition, her hair had started to fall out, leading to her being sent to see a specialist. However, no reason or explanation was given other than she was to stop drying her hair over the gas fire.

After coming out of Nazareth House eight years previously, we were sensitive children, and although in those earlier years we would not have been aware of it, our subconscious beliefs would have been deeply affected. Family life has a massive impact on a child's well-being. Nowadays, it is well documented that economic hardship and maternal depression can affect children's brain activity and stress hormone levels. Gilly felt this tension the most when Mam metered out her own brand of discipline, whether verbally or physically. Her thoughts and imaginings had her believing we were adopted, and she was always waiting for her real Mam to turn up. Later in life, Gilly had to take to the fact that we were already living with our natural parents. Back then, children's mental health issues were taken less seriously, and many concerns were *swept under the carpet*. Our parents' type of parenting was *authoritarian*, strict and insisting their orders be obeyed. Mam especially showed low levels of warmth, with them both expecting us to behave. I now know from personal

Nazareth House Card

experience that parenting is not easy. Mam lacked any support structure around her and must have breathed a sigh of relief when Dad took us all out to the park to play football with other kids in the road. Back in *the good old days*, we were left to play outside in the close until dark, and some children had much more freedom than we did, only having to be home before the streetlights came on. Other adults would reprimand us if we didn't show good manners and respect for our elders. Even the police, the local priest and the nuns in school disciplined the unruly children. Grownups were in charge, no question, and with that came a created sense of stability, sometimes good and sometimes bad, but it kept the world spinning. As children, we felt the constant need to ask permission, requiring reassurance from those adults within our circle. Hypercritical adults cause children to internalise damaging mindsets. I have always struggled with the word *obedience*, linking it to punishment, maybe wrongly thinking that we were disobedient and sent to the children's home.

I personally grew up with a fear of failure as hanging onto the past sometimes causes deep shame. People reading this book may dismiss these childhood fears but, believe me, these are very real in the lives of the children who have passed through the doors of Nazareth House or through the care system.

I want to be open and vulnerable by giving snapshots of events in my life that may be poorly framed but will, hopefully, help other people who have been through care of any kind to understand that they can stop reliving past pain. We have all been through cruel and distressing situations that we are not proud of or happy with, which sadly is a part of life.

Like me, have you believed lies, which in turn have created fear? Have you had a hypercritical upbringing? Causing worry, anxiety, doubt, fear of failure, self-effort, health problems, unforgiveness and control? These are powerless ghosts holding you shackled in chains of oppression from which you CAN be set free. You can receive *heart healing.*

The Bible (Amplified version) states in Isiah 26:14:

"They (the former tyrant masters) are dead, they shall not live and reappear; they are powerless ghosts, they shall not rise and come back. Therefore You (God) have visited and made an end of them and caused every memory of them (every trace of their supremacy) to PERISH."

Bible reading: The Passion Version
MATTHEW Chapter 11, Verses 28-30

"Are you weary, carrying a heavy burden?
Then come to me. (Jesus).
I will refresh your life, for I AM your oasis.
Simply join your life with mine.
Learn my ways and you'll discover that I'm
Gentle, humble, easy to please.
You will find refreshment and rest in me.
For all that I require of you will be
Pleasant and easy to bear."

A friend of mine, Celia, challenged me in April 2020 saying I was still living in the past, carrying burdens that were pulling me down. This honesty had me make a list of emotions I felt at that time. Can you figure out where your own personal fear has come from? Naming the fear takes away some of its power. FEAR = false evidence appearing real.

I was over-identifying with failure, believing this book would not be as good as *3 Peas in a Pram.* However, regardless of my upbringing and fear of failure, I have realised this is an opportunity for growth, not a death sentence for *3 Peas in the 70s.* Writing this section has taken me out of my comfort zone. I found encouragement during a dream about Nazareth House. In my dream, I was holding the hand of a nun, helping her step down from a bus as there were big rocks on the ground below her. Stepping through the doors of Nazareth House, I looked in the first room on my right. I could see two rows of babies, fast asleep, in what looked like clear, plastic sledges. They were all packed in tightly against each other. All was quiet. I carried on walking and saw that in the second room, there were beds up and down each side of the room, packed in tightly. The children were fast asleep. Still, walking on, I came to a third room. I could see young women making jam sandwiches – I just stood, quietly watching. Suddenly, I was back outside the home, waving goodbye to the same nun I had helped off the bus. She turned and said, "After talking to you, you have done something to me." I woke up. Since having that dream, I have been able for the first time in my life to imagine what life may have been like during our stay there in the 1960s. Realising that the truth was, we were cared for as best as those around us could do. With so many other needy children around them, people were overwhelmed with these children's needs and cries for comfort.

I have had to travel these recent experiences to enable me to give the following account: Remembering gave me an ache in my heart, and I could hear the words spoken by a nun, "take them upstairs to the nursery". I could feel tears welling up, and I was suddenly that little four-year-old girl kicking and screaming about being left there by the welfare. Unable to do anything about our year-long stay in the children's home, real fear and frustration rose in me, coming from being unable to control these events around me. We had a new routine of everyday events occupying our days – some so alien to our previous care that they would have taken some getting used to. More questions were rising up until a thought broke through of each passing day, bringing us closer to Dad's promise that he would come back and collect us to take us home. Eventually, a year later, in July 1962, he did. I can imagine him walking us through Albert Park, with us three skipping happily alongside him, to start the next chapter of our lives.

I sensed the Heavenly Father saying, "Tell people that I walked the corridors of Nazareth House every night, touching the heads of every child, bringing peace in their storm of life. Some children, like your sister Francy, sensed my presence, but others were unable to feel my touch because of their pain. Just like during your time in the children's home, I am still in control of your life and the events that surround you. Give me the frustration and the anger. You are on a journey with me alongside you. Do I not promise I will never leave you nor forsake you?"

God has been the Champion of all the children, past and present, who lived through those experiences with part of their lives in Nazareth House, or in the care system. I understand that some other children have been less fortunate in the way they were cared for. I believe my dream was given to help me to pray for peace and freedom for those babies, children, and young women.

You, too, may think you were being punished for being disobedient and therefore sent to a children's home as a consequence. THIS IS NOT TRUE! Neither you nor I have found our journey easy, but may I ask you a question? Are you still living in the past? If the answer is yes, my prayer is for you to know a new freedom and that the dark shadow of the Nazareth House building will be demolished by a large wrecking ball, no longer being a part of your landscape.

I hope my personal account inspires you to have a better understanding of the memories of your past. I've read somewhere that worry can become a habit

(Oops, no pun intended if you are a nun). Maybe this moment is for you to break the habit of a lifetime. Jesus says, "Follow me. Are you tired? Worn out? Burned out on religion? Come to me. Get away with me, and you will recover your life. I'll show you how to take a real rest. Walk with me and work with me and watch how I do it. Learn the unforced rhythms of grace. I won't lay anything heavy or ill-fitting on you. Keep company with me, and you'll learn to live freely and lightly".

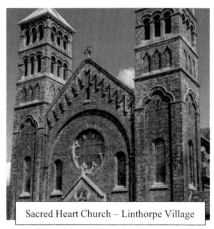

Sacred Heart Church – Linthorpe Village

Jesus doesn't offer us an escape but the equipment of an easy yoke. Life at his pace – slow, unhurried, full of love, joy and peace. Your choice.

Some may find this chapter challenging to read due to personal experiences or from living through lockdown. Or perhaps the reason may be as simple as you are *stuck*. Stuck in the doldrums. This is a nautical term where ships get stuck in windless waters. Because of the Covid virus, people who are not on the frontline have been asked to remain at home. It has therefore been quiet, with nothing new or exciting happening.

This state of inactivity has an effect similar to listlessness or stagnation, where sail-powered boats are trapped for days or weeks. In this stillness, I personally have been mourning how I've expected life to be before this virus. There has been the little four-year-old girl in me, still struggling to cope with everything going on around me. The deaths being tallied each day and the prayer requests have been overwhelming. Anxiety, stress, and fear have all been revealing their ugly heads. Childish fears have filled my thoughts, making me think that everyone I know, and love, will die. Why should it surprise me that my past needed to be dealt with when the world is in such turmoil? I have had health problems and disappointments, all due to social distancing, but I have learnt the hard way that the key has been in *resting*. May I suggest you use this time wisely to declutter the rubbish and guilt from the past, to enable you to walk into the future, post-pandemic, with peace in your heart? Have you wanted to write a letter, a poem, a book, paint or take up another creative pastime? Do it. You may hold a gift to bless future generations to ease their way in life and encourage them in the uncertain future ahead.

Maybe you could do what the Psalmist did:

*"I lift my eyes to the hills
Where does my help come from?
My help comes from the Lord,
The maker of heaven and earth."*

Back in October 1971, a family moved into 15 Hereford Close. Staunch Catholics, Mr and Mrs Greenheld, had five children, all of which were boys. In the years ahead, they would be looking and praying to God for help in their worst nightmare. David, their youngest son, would be found to have childhood cancer. Our families settled into a happy routine of building friendship ties, often found in each other's houses. I remember these times having quite a sad feeling, little knowing the worry and heartache this family was travelling through and not understanding why David looked so pale and ill. Eventually, *the cat was let out the bag*, revealing the previously hidden cause.

Like the subject of death, this disease was rarely spoken about, let alone discussed. David was often absent from school in the fear he would pick up germs and infections, especially during his cancer treatments. I remember him standing outside his house just watching us all playing in the sunshine. This young lad's health continued to deteriorate with him once again in bed over Christmas time in 1975. Mam wrote to Dad in January 1976 letting him know:

"David Greenheld went into hospital last week. He was in bed poorly over New Year, and the doctor found he had a chest infection. He is on tablets and injections, and this is slowly clearing up. His mum and I went to see him last Saturday, and he was very drowsy but looked a bit better. He said the hospital food was horrible. I took him some Lucozade and some detective books, and he was really pleased with these."

Dad also received a letter from David's older brother, Gerard, in early February telling him:

"I am sorry it is so long since I last wrote to you but know you will understand. You will by now have heard about David. It is so sad and as hit me hard as I did not know how ill he was 'til two days ago, before he passed away

when my father told me, he did not have long to live."

Sadly, it appears David didn't come out of hospital and died in late January, causing both Mam and I to set pen to paper to keep Dad updated. Mam's airmail states:

"Well, things are slowly getting back to normal after last week's tragedy. The Greenheld boys have been coming in our house every evening for an hour or two. Little Norman and I have been playing dominoes (1p a game), and guess who won the jackpot?"

I wrote:

"The Greedheld's are still recovering from David's death. Anthony and Norman seem much the same as usual, though they all feel they have been hit hard.
I keep popping in and out to see everyone to try and cheer them up a bit. I went in last night about 10:15pm to get some sugar, everyone had gone to bed except the dad and Alan. So, I sat listening to Alan pouring out his troubles about how he is going to change his job. You'd be proud of how Mam has coped with the whole family. I don't know what they would have done without her."

That New Year brought trouble to several houses in Hereford Close – Dad was informed:

"You will be sorry to hear Arthur Murray is in trouble again. On Monday night we heard this commotion and people rushed out on their doorsteps. Arthur had a big piece of wood and smashed the front door in and the panes of glass down the side. Mrs Murray was in the O'Connor's house at the time, and they called the police, who spoke to him in the house. About an hour later, he went round the back of the house and smashed the door and the windows in. Then the police came and took him away. He was remanded for 7 days for reports. Mrs Murray has gone to stay at Mary's, and she will have to pay for these herself. Isn't this heart-breaking for her?"

This airmail was quickly followed with a further update:

"Continuing the story of Hereford Close (or Coronation Street of Cleveland). Following Arthur Murray's little escapade, we had two fire engines and police cars down here in the early hours of the morning, dealing with a fire at Kenny's house down the bottom. His stepfather was away at relations and Kenny was on night shift. The house is ruined, all the windows are out, and all the furniture is burnt and just thrown in the garden. The place was swarming with CID men…and now we have two houses in the road boarded up!"

The Murray's house was next door to ours and no doubt we will have felt scared with Arthur Murray's violent outbursts. I clearly remember Mrs Murray banging on our door and shouting that Arthur had slashed his wrists. Dad raced to their house and had to break down the bathroom door. He bandaged this young man's wrists and waited for the ambulance. Clearly, he had mental health issues and was taken to the hospital. Back in his own house, Dad was shaking as he recounted what had happened. He had to get bathed and changed, and he was covered in blood. Not something you would forget in a hurry. I can recall Dad was very kind to both the Greenheld and Murray families, often walking their dogs and, if needed, doing one-off jobs for them.

People have different ways of coping with life events, and our cousin, Martin, was no exception. Martin became one of the family after Aunty Katy and Uncle Les adopted him as a baby. I remember a card came through the letterbox inviting our household to his baptism, causing me to quiz Mam on how this baby could have arrived without Aunty Katy having a bump.

Having no personal experience to draw upon bringing up children, Katy read up on Dr Spock's book *The Common Book of Baby and Child Care*. Spock encouraged fathers to play an active role in raising their children. Parents were to trust their instincts and feed babies if they were hungry outside the prescribed eating times. It taught that parents should show their babies love. What seems perfectly normal advice now was completely revolutionary at the time. Thus, the entire baby boom generation was raised on this new softer approach to parenting. Some blamed Dr Spock for the unruly anti-government youth of the 1960s. This book completely changed the way parents raised their offspring, having elements of good old-fashioned common sense. Martin was raised on this much-loved book, which was everywhere. It has sold more than fifty million copies worldwide since its first publication back in 1946.

Although raised by loving parents, Martin in his teenage years, began to cause angst and persistent worry, often recorded by Mam:

"Katy couldn't get up to see your dad this week because of the trouble with Martin. On Wednesday a policeman knocked on the door and asked me if I knew the whereabouts of Martin. Apparently, he had run away from home, taking some money out of the bureau. I phoned Katy, of course, and on Friday she told me he had made his way to Leamington Spa – to Robin of all people. He just will not go to school. Your Colin brought him home on the train last Tuesday and he just stays in his room. Katy is waiting to hear from the education authority. Such a worry for her and Les. They should be able to do something to help them, I think."

In the April of 1976, Mam wrote concerning a visit from Martin:

"On Wednesday, Martin came down as it was his birthday. I bought him a little present, and he got a cassette recorder from his parents. He was in a funny mood as he had nowhere to go and of course there was no party for him. Anyway, he got shouted at a couple of times as he has to toe the line in our house."

Eventually, later in life, this once troublesome young man developed into a loving son. Aunty Katy began to suffer a series of strokes. She was then looked after at home by her devoted husband, Les, with Martin having a supporting role by their sides.

Some families have a life of setbacks and adversity, and the Greedhelds continued suffering ill-health after experiencing the loss of David, with Mam letting Dad know:

"Things are back to normal in our house at the moment, though we have the Greenhelds popping in most of the time. I think the boys are glad of the noise and normality of our family as their parents are still very depressed, which is only natural.*"*

In March, Mam was still in her supporting role, stating:

"I had a nice day on Thursday. Mrs G and I went down to town and had a lovely time strolling around the shops looking at all the ladies' clothes. She treated herself to some trousers and then we went for a bite to eat. I could see her visibly cheering up as time went on."

Clearly, Gerald's health was suffering as I wrote to Dad on 9.3.76 saying:

"Ged (Greenheld) has started to dig the left side of our garden up; he's going to plant spuds and other things. He only has to lift the spade once and he's breathless. He has got the sack and worked a weeks' notice. I'm not surprised as he would not get up in the
mornings and kept having days off!"

Writing up this chapter, the penny dropped as to why my mother suffered from depression. So affected by David's death, supporting his family in the aftermath, Dad working away, and her daughters all living out life's dramas took a toll on her mental health. Though Mam would certainly attest to people needing life experiences, even the hard knocks, calling it *character building*.

I came across a poem titled, *Life of Hard Knocks* by Ray Hansell, which sums up this chapter on worry perfectly.

As I walk down life's road
I, like anyone have regrets
There are so many things in life
That I'd like to forget

Those times when things went wrong
As they sometimes will
All the mistakes that I make
Especially the ones that haunt me still

Not every road walked was smooth
Some were filled with potholes and bumps
But just like everyone else
In life I took my lumps

I never did complain
I thought, what's the use
Because when people hear you
They think you're just making an excuse

So, as you travel down life's road
You should always remember
That in this life of hard knocks
Every one of us is a member.

Chapter Three - Wealth

As I settled down to write this chapter, a song, *Sunrise, Sunset*, came to mind. This is a wedding song from the musical *Fiddler on the Roof*, written in 1964 by composer Jerry Bock and lyricist Sheldon Harnick. Two parents sang about how they can't believe their daughter and groom have grown up so swiftly flow the years. How true, as I now find myself writing social history spanning three generations. The parents continue singing, asking, "What words of wisdom can I give them? How can I help ease their way?" Isn't that a gift one generation would like to leave for the generation of the future? Words of wisdom. Easing their way by sharing life's experiences – the good and the bad told with honesty and a healthy dose of forgiveness thrown in?

So, back to social history.

The term 'teenager' was first used in America in 1941, defining young people between 13 and 19. My mother, Irene, was a teenager in the 1940s, I was a teenager in the 1970s, and my daughter, Jenny, was a teenager in the 2000s. In the 1940s, food would have been rationed, both during and after the war. Food was actually more strictly controlled in the post-war years. Tea was rationed until 1952, which may explain our love affair as a *tea drinking nation*. Bread, potatoes and bananas were also in short supply, with clothing taken off the rationing list on 31.09.1949. Growing up in the 1960s and 1970s, our food was rationed too. We had to ask permission to obtain food from the pantry. The four of us had healthy appetites and would be like a hoard of locusts eating anything in sight. Our parents' attitude only improved once we started paying £5 rent a week. Mam was also selective in feeding Dad the best quality food. He ate steak and butter, we had sausages and margarine. Whereas my children practically had free rein of the food cupboards. However, our families placed high importance on wellness in all three generations – a balanced diet alongside healthy lifestyles. We have had a preference for *all things British*, supporting local shops around the areas where we lived.

Some British brand names have also stood the test of time within our family's eating habits. One brand will be of no surprise – Farrows Giant Marrowfat Processed Peas. As a child, I remember the slogan that advertised this tastiest pea that you can put on your plate: A crow lands on a fence and goes, "Squark, where is my dinner?" A voice replies, "Sorry mate, you're too late. All the best peas have gone to Farrows."

This company claimed to be the first business in England to sell dried peas in packets. Then in 1930, aided by the development of pea harvesting machinery, began canning Farrow peas.

After wisely acquiring Gale & Co Ltd, this firm had a growth in popularity. Years later, this special brand of pea was sold on to Princes Foods in Liverpool in 2011 and is still in production today.

As I was thinking about why certain foods span generations, the word 'comfort' came to mind. These kinds of food provide a nostalgic or sentimental value to us as individuals. We often associate these products with childhood or home cooking.

Lyles golden syrup was another favourite choice, especially pleasing poured over pancakes and had its own unique flavour. More than a million tins leave the bank of the River Thames each month, going to all the four corners of the globe – from America, Yemen, China, South Africa and Australia. The design on this tin remains the same today (the lion and the bees), with Guinness World Records confirming this as the oldest unchanged brand packaging since it took shape in 1883.

During my research on this logo, I came across this poem called *Sampson's Lion* which is reproduced on the next page.

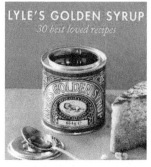

One treat my daughter Jenny missed out on was collecting Golly badges from Robertson's brand of Golden Shred Marmalade. These pin badges appeared in England in the 1920s and were fun to collect and swap with friends for a large part of our childhood. Nearly all the money raised on these badges and memorabilia was donated to charities this company supported.

Golly was a black-faced golliwog figure with frizzy hair, white eyes, and red lips. Sadly, back in 1983, the Greater London council opted to boycott Robertson's mascot and product as offensive. This beloved icon who stood for healthy eating, recycling and children's safety was retired in 2002. Instead, characters from the Roald Dahl series of books were used in promotional advertising.

Previous generations were caught up collecting these badges, with breakfast consisting of bread toasted by the fire covered only with Robertson's marmalade, bringing happiness to many hungry children. Once founded in 1864, the sale of Golden Shred Marmalade has now been taken over by Premier Foods. A sad end for the once-famous nursery land character of the Robertson's fame.

The shopping experience has been very different through our own family's generations. Francy recalls traipsing around all the shops in Linthorpe Village with Mam, hunting for all the bargains, hoping to find items a penny cheaper. Walking to the stores in the village nearly every day, found one of us in tow with her to help carry the shopping home. Mam was always weary and needed to stop often, weighed down with fresh fruit and vegetables. Mam lived in a world where pizzas, McDonalds and instant coffee were not part of her life; all meals were homemade and took a large chunk of time in her day-to-day chores. She thought fast food was what you ate at Lent, a Big Mac was an oversized coat, and a crumpet was what we had for tea. I remember being sent to the neighbours' doors to ask if we could borrow an egg or a cup of sugar when money was in short supply. The favour would be reciprocated in their time of need.

My personal experience also includes shopping locally, especially after the children were born. We now lived in an outer suburb of the town of Middlesbrough in Nunthorpe. This boasted a parade of local amenities, including a newsagent, bank, post office, pharmacy, bread shop, a butcher and back then, a Hinton's store, making this an attractive place to live. Saturdays found the children and I visiting my parents, whilst David went to the local Boro matches. I would wander with Mam to the village to top up on any shopping needed for the weekend. As I was no longer working, we decided to trim the bills and switch to cheaper brands. We now shopped in Netto and other cheaper shops, trying out store-branded goods.

The lion that on Sampson roared
And thirsted for his blood.
With honey afterwards was stored,
And furnished him with food

Believers, as they pace along,
With many lions meet;
But gather sweetness from the strong,
And from the eater, meat

The lions rage and roar in vain,
For Jesus is their shield;
Their losses prove a certain gain,
Their troubles comfort yield

The world and Satan join their strength
To fill their soul with fears;
But crops of joy they reap at length
From what they sow in tears

Afflictions make them love the word,
Stir up their hearts to prayer;
And many precious proofs afford,
Of their Redeemers care

The lions roar but cannot kill,
Then fear them not, my friends,
They bring us, though against their will
The honey Jesus sends

John Newton

We discovered that not all the brand names were necessarily better quality. Some of the foods have come out of the same factories, therefore having the same ingredients inside. The only difference is the packaging. I remember being really surprised when David told me this. Why wouldn't people swap to a store brand when it means they're able to save maybe 30% off their shopping bill? Definitely food for thought. Even now, though, I still enjoy the taste of branded foods like Heinz tomato soup, Kellogg's cornflakes and Jacob's cream crackers with butter.

Rosemary stood outside 19 Hereford Close, 19 years old

My daughter has the choice to shop locally, visit supermarkets, or even now have the luxury of shopping online from the comfort of her own home. Her food is then delivered to her door. Unthinkable two generations previously, for those who were born before television, dishwashers, and tumble dryers.

Back in the 1950s, housewives could spend up to 15 hours a day on domestic chores. Only about 4% of British households owned a washing machine. Back then, washing was always done on a Monday. Most women thought cleanliness was next to godliness, with this extending to net curtains, blankets, sheets and clothes all being washed by hand, with the water being boiled first.

Francy vividly remembers Mam washing and turning the hand crank to wring out the excess water. No wonder women had no time to cook a meal – so Monday's dinner was leftover food from Sunday.

After moving to Hereford Close, our parents purchased a twin tub washing machine. This was versatile and economical. Simply fill one of the tubs with water from the hot tap with the pipe provided, then wash, rinse and use the other tub to spin the moisture out. This was my first washing machine as well, inherited from my mother-in-law in 1980.

Inside Hereford Close, 1976

Launderettes became popular in the 1960s, with over 12,000 nationwide in the 1980s. Domestic washing machines were expensive and unreliable, often breaking down, so using the *washeteria* was cost-effective. Just bring the washing, put it in the self-service coin machine and wait. When household appliances became cheaper, the launderettes reduced in numbers to three thousand. However, many of us still use one of these preserved laundrettes for various reasons. Personally, I use them to wash modern duvets and quilts – too big for my domestic machine.

Amazingly, the first-ever self-service outdoor launderette in Bestwood, Nottingham, opened in May 2014. The *Revolution 24* is open 24/7 so customers can wash and shop at the same time. I wonder what Mam would have thought about that. She was born before the 1940s, before dishwashers, tumble dryers and drip-dry clothes. No wonder she would get confused, saying there is a generation gap. She would say the world was a kinder place back in her day. Neighbours helped one another, especially in a crisis. Older, ill parents would come to live with the next of kin, with my generation having great respect for elders and grandparents. Grandad George came to live with our family for a short period to give my Aunty Katy a rest from having him living with her family full time. One morning, Grandad was up early, and my sister was preparing the paper and sticks to start the coal fire. She looked up, and Grandad had his long johns on back to front. All she could think about was how upset he would be if he couldn't use the toilet properly. So, she helped him switch his underwear the other way round – an experience she has never forgotten. Grandad would go from house to house until going to live in a home.

Doors were never locked; maybe people were more trustworthy, or perhaps we had less money. Most of it was spent on food and bills. They didn't buy what they couldn't afford. They just did without. Everyone was in the same boat. The holes in the settee would be covered. Mam used to dream of living in a country cottage with roses around the door, but it was not to be. Later in life, they would actually look into buying their rented council property but never took up this golden opportunity. In 1979, council tenants were given the right to buy their homes under the new housing bill. The government was sure this new policy would be extremely popular. It proved to be so, with over 400,000 tenants taking advantage of this new progressive structure. At this time, there were still the haves and have nots within the community, so this policy paved the way for property-owning equality and improved the social structure for good. Fortunately, during this period, Dad was employed by Kearns Barker Associates as a site foreman from February 1978 to August 1980. This company was based at Bishopton Lane, Stockton-on-Tees, in Cleveland.

One warm summer's day, Dad came through the back door with a little white and black kitten cradled in his arm. The cat at work had had a set of kittens that needed new homes. Once placed on the kitchen floor, this tiny little creature squeezed under the cooker to hide. This was how it was decided; her name was to be Heidi. Over the next few days, Heidi spent more time hiding under the washer and would only be seen when hungry. Saucers of milk and little titbits were fed to her as she settled in her new home. Then, growing in confidence, she began exploring the garden, pouncing on anything that moved. She was given a collar to wear with a bell to stop her catching birds or mice that she often brought to Mam as a gift.

Heidi loved Mam, maybe because she was the one to feed her – she could be found rubbing up against her owner's legs as a form of cupboard love, to get food or attention. This cat would sit on Dad's papers, sleep on their bed and sharpen its claws on the chairs or wallpaper. She roamed outside and once disappeared for a few days, to be found as a stray living in a neighbour's house at the top of our road. Heidi was our property and had to be returned to number 19, much to this lady's dismay. Sitting on the window ledge outside, she would meow until the door was opened for her to jump down and be let in. Once in summer, two other cats followed her in. They shared her food on the saucer and then disappeared. After being let out one night, Heidi didn't return. The following morning Dad went looking for her and found her tucked away under a bush. Carrying her back in the house, he said it looked like she had been run over by a car. After a trip to the vets, she came back with a plaster cast on her back leg that had been broken in the accident. Looking very sorry for herself, she slept a lot over the following days, but soon she was managing to get up and down the stairs, looking very comical as she dragged the pot down each stair with a *thump, thump, thump*. Heidi had a comfortable, sometimes pampered, life living in the Farrow family but had a real dislike of the grandchildren, putting them in their place by scratching them. Both Gilly and Francy said having a cat at home sparked their love of all things feline, whereas I can take them or leave them – another difference between my sisters and me.

However, I have always viewed being a triplet as a blessing and one of the greatest joys in my life. We have been best friends from the womb, and I have loved sharing life with these amazing sisters of mine, even to the point (back then) of wanting us all to live together when we got married. In hindsight, this was very unrealistic and would not have been a good idea.

Being triplets went through stages, with the main hurdle to grow in confidence when your close siblings were not around. We began to live this experience only when starting St Thomas' senior school, and it was terrifying. At the age of eleven, we were placed in different classes causing the three of us extreme panic and may be termed as now *separation anxiety*.

The only thing I ever wanted to do differently to my sisters was to wear different coloured clothing to them. Independence took many years to achieve and was a painful process. We learned the lessons of being comfortable alone and trusting others around us. We still suffered from name labelling – with Francy being called *kind*, Gilly *clever* and me *cheeky*. Gilly recalls me as having a happy and sunny disposition that rubbed off on those around me. Sometimes helping me when faced with tough times. By the time we entered the convent at thirteen years of age, we were used to being in different parts of the school but were always on the lookout for each other in the corridors. Francy remembers her heart leaping for joy when we spied one another. We were always happy to be back together in each other's company. Sometimes (in a nice way), we would blackmail one another into doing things, accepting one another with unconditional love, most of the time.

A lovely trait of being part of a multiple birth was an unspoken ability to be willing to share. However, the line was drawn in the sand in sharing boyfriends. These lads would have to pass this triplet test. Occasionally there was a mix-up. One evening in the dim light of the TV, one lad found his arms wrapped around the wrong triplet, causing a laugh, much to his embarrassment.

Being one of three also brought out a competitive streak in us. Looking back, it spurred us on to try to be the best we could possibly be. We were so in tune with one another, relying emotionally and mentally within this unique relationship.

I love sharing with people that I am a triplet and have been asked all sorts of questions over the years – some rude and some stupid. But the main one being, can we feel each other's pain? For me personally, the answer is no. But Gilly and Francy have a type of sixth sense with one another. Dad would tell the story of us as young babies where he had put us all down to sleep for the night. However, Gilly wouldn't stop crying. He came back to our room. He saw Francy had turned blue and scooping her up, he ran to the nearest red phone box. After speaking to the doctor, he was told to wait where he was. The doctor came back to him. Gilly saved her sister's life that night. This ability to *know* something also came to light years later when Gilly gave birth to her first son, Mark. Francy remembers feeling upset, sensing something was really wrong and thinking, would she ever see Gilly again? After being given an epidural, Gilly had a severe reaction to the additives in this medication but thankfully survived due to the quick response of a nurse at Parkside Maternity. We had to wait two full days before we were allowed to visit, and only then was Francy's anxiety relieved to see her younger triplet alive.

These chinks in our armour sometimes made us vulnerable to the outside world, as well as emotionally. I remember often being upset when people didn't take the time to actually look at us, just seeing us as an entity, before using the first name that came to mind, usually the wrong one.

Dad always worked through all his daughters' names before finishing by saying, "You are my favourite daughter." You couldn't help but burst out laughing. We must have been very alike as no one noticed my two sisters changing places in their art and history lessons in the convent, later changing classes again, with no one any the wiser. Boys would always stare at the three of us, and Mam said we were like traffic lights, always blushing and turning red from their unwanted gaze. Heaven only knows what was going through their minds. We were always visible and really had nowhere to hide. Francy was painfully shy, and the three of us came across as quite timid in certain situations, but we always had a close bond with each other, helping us to have someone to share and enjoy life with.

When we started work, the gifts of sharing and listening spilt out into the lives of the women in each of our places of work. I was often sent to the women's toilets after someone burst out crying to be a listening ear and offer comfort where I could. Good listeners might be the term used today. We had a natural warmth and friendliness inherited from our dad.

Sometimes we would voice our worries for our sisters in an excessive way, causing David to comment, "The only time you triplets, as people, could have an understanding for an individual's life, is when you become independent of one another". That was difficult, always watching each other's backs in agreement on lots of things and often living in each other's pockets. We lived together – therefore, we saw no harm in being dependent on one another as it was a way of life for us – finishing each other's sentences, with memories always in plural.

Why would you not want to spend time with triplet sisters who understood you completely? Where you were quickly forgiven for any petty offence, held in affection without limitations by two other girls who looked identical to yourself?

The obvious downside to bringing up triplet daughters back in the 1970s was that our parents didn't have much spare money. So, we never went on school trips, whether home or abroad, as providing the funds for the three of us was impossible. But our younger sister, Ann, fared much better in that department, often travelling with school or her friends.

Sharing is caring in this multiple bond. I hope I have given you an insight into the behind-the-scenes experiences from our viewpoint. Our cousin, Anthony, recalls we had a closeness, always talking and gossiping with a steady stream of conversation. We were different because we were *very open*, whereas it is more natural for other people to be private. So, it was us that was different. I think this is an interesting observation from him. It is our openness that God uses to help us relate to people around us. This, in turn, allows them to share their lives and problems.

This has been nostalgic for me, recalling this wealth of happy, personal memories. I would like to finish this chapter by letting you know I stopped going to the Boro matches after my nephew, Mark, was born in July 1981. It was much more enjoyable cuddling a brand-new baby. I picked up my knitting needles and began a love affair of producing bespoke baby outfits, which has spilt over the years to knitting for grandchildren in the present day.

Chapter Four – Worship

A s a child, the word worship immediately brought to mind a Catholic song titled, *The Ten Commandments*. Neither the author nor the composer is known.

First, I must honour God
Second, honour his name
Third, on His day be holy, this will be my aim
Fourth, I must be obedient
Fifth, be kind and true
Sixth, be pure in all I say and see and hear and do
Seventh, I must be honest
Eighth, be truthful in all things I say
Ninth, be pure in mind and heart and all I think and desire each day
Tenth, I must be satisfied, not be jealous, come what may.
These are God's Ten Commandments. These I must obey.

This song can be summed up in a modern version of these two golden Commandments:
- LOVE – Love the Lord your God with every passion of your heart, with all the energy of your being and with every thought that is within you.
- You must LOVE your friend in the same way you love yourself.

So, part of our worship, as young girls and teenagers, involved singing in two choirs, which we all equally enjoyed. The choir master at Sacred Heart Church in those days was Mr Austin Mylia. He taught us The Ave Maria set to a moving

Sunday Service Circa 1971

tune by Franz Schubert. I have only realised the words in English are taken from a humble Catholic prayer, The Hail Mary.

We were taught by rote. This means we learnt maths, history, songs and school subjects parrot-fashion, without thinking, only having a retention of what had been entrusted to memory. We were like sponges soaking up the music of the time. An older lady, Joan Harkin, recalls, this church choir would venture out at Christmastime to sing in old people's homes. She too was educated at the convent, saying, "On choir days at the convent, I took a packed lunch. We were allowed to eat in a classroom, but we had to provide a tablecloth to cover the desks."

Years later, my sisters and I loved being a part of the school's choir too, even though we sometimes felt on display. Blonde Mrs Schoenburg was our music teacher and took a shine to the three of us. Although we didn't have the ability to read the notes on the music sheets, we followed the notes up and down and quickly picked up the tune of new songs. One of the girls, Anne Bowman, told me, one of her memories was the beauty of our voices. We were so talented. Poor Anne was desperate to be a part of the ensemble of singers but didn't have a good musical voice. One day the music teacher was running late and asked for girls to sing in groups of three. She found herself wedged between her friend Nadine and my sister Francy and lip-synced to the song. To her joy, she heard the teacher say, "Good, you are all in.".

Being a part of this choir also allowed Francy, Gilly and me to be together, which could never be often enough, as three was never a crowd. It was like this is what we were born to do – sing together – as our voices naturally harmonised perfectly.

Mrs Schoenburg recognised our *God-given ability*. She taught us to sing *Three Little Maids from School* from the Mikado, perfect for a beginning vocal trio. However, stood on the stage in front of parents and pupils, both Francy and Gilly had a case of stage fright. Another girl had to stand in – an experience they would both rather forget.

We were soon back singing with our usual gusto – singing joyful, challenging music from operettas, folk, gospel, pop or hymns. It was worth all the hard work of practising as we had time off school lessons to enter competitions. Travelling by bus to Whitby and Billingham were moments fuelled with adventure, as the choir grew in confidence, often beating stiff competition and returning to the girls' school clutching winning trophies.

Choirs from all over the country took part in the Hallelujah Chorus in Billingham – Francy recalls taking part, singing the descant. This is like a second song, set apart from the main melody, and we had to watch our music teacher for a cue to sing *our part*.

Interestingly, we started to recognise a difference in social class around this time, with other girls from well-to-do areas now a part of our lives. In our eyes, these young ladies were well dressed, in the correct uniform, spoke in posh voices and came from posh detached houses. Whereas our background, coming from a council estate, meant we spoke in a local Boro accent and, because our parents struggled financially, felt we were never dressed in the complete uniform. I think this caused us to feel that, in general, we were never accepted or approved of, causing us mainly to mix with our friends from a similar background. All our friends were white working class, and I only remember a couple of girls with brown skin – Nadine being one of them – within our classrooms.

Looking back, our parents' generation would have been classed as racist.

Sadly, I think this is a trait passed from one generation to another, resulting in prejudice towards people based on their race or ethnicity. We had no awareness of how other social groups lived their cultural tradition. Neither was this taught in the education system – they were like little mushrooms kept in the dark.

We continued attending church well into our late teens. I hold an airmail letter dated 11.1.76 stating:

"We had a good sing at church today, I really enjoyed it. Mr Mylia has asked us to sing for the old people next Sunday at about 3.30pm. Guess what we are singing, well surprise, surprise… Moonlight and Roses and Cockles and Mussels. I hope they like it."

All the airmail letters have been signed and finished with references to prayer or terms of endearment, like:

Your ever-loving Rosie
All my love, Irene
God bless and keep you safe, your lovely Rosie x
Your ever-loving daughter, Francy x
Always loving you, Snug (Ann's nickname)

With a quote:

"Soft and bright and full of living
Is the soul that's really free,
Jesus speaks the answers clearly
Find yourself in loving me
God bless, take care, thinking about
you, all my love, Gill

We would write and say that we had lit a candle in church and were praying for him. I wonder if Dad realised how much he was loved and missed by his family whilst working away.

Each week, people gathered together for another cause, singing their hearts out, clapping and 'worshipping' their local football team. My boyfriend David was no exception, introducing me to the enjoyment of this sport.

Mam wrote to Dad stating:

"Rosie is going around with David Gott, and they have started going to football matches!!"

I wrote to Dad, giving more details:

"Guess where I went on Tuesday night? To the Boro match against Manchester City. Don't worry I didn't come to any harm. Dave looked after me, we got to the gate about 7:10pm and there were long lines of men waiting to get into the match. When we were nearly to the pay box, everyone started to push the people at the front I was a bit scared, and Dave kept asking if I was all right. He asked the man in front to let me get by – it was a tight squeeze, but I was in! After that, I enjoyed being there. It was quite an experience. There was no trouble that I know of except a stupid Boro fan threw an empty bottle at our goalie. Nothing came of this. We were definitely the better team even though we missed scoring three goals in the first half; I thought they were never going to get a goal! In the second half, Hickton scored the only goal of the match, The Boro crowd went mad, they all seemed to grow and close into one another, like some great mass.
They also turned about 4,000 away from the gates. The grounds were full to busting! Does it hold 34,000 or 38,000? Hope you are not mad at me for going 'cos I really enjoyed myself and I said to Dave you should have been there as well. I'm so sad you weren't."

Mam knew Dad enjoyed hearing about his local football team. She wrote a couple more times keeping him up to date on his daughters' involvement too:

"Snug and her Dave went with Rosie and David on Tuesday night, and Snug really enjoyed herself Tony MacAndrew has been in the team recently and seems to be playing well."

"Have you heard any news about the Boro yet? They have signed on a new player, Phil Boersma, for £70,000. He played against Manchester last week and had a good game.
Boro also played Fulham and beat them 1-0 through an own goal, so they have now won the Anglo Scottish Cup!"

My father supported Middlesbrough Football Club that has the nickname *The Boro*. This club was founded back in 1876, and since 1899, the home kit comprised a red shirt with white detailing, shorts, and either red or white socks. Jack Charlton (the Manager) introduced a broad white stripe across the chest, often favoured by the local supporters in 1973.

My brother-in-law, Robert, was an avid Boro supporter alongside his mam, Sally and his nana. Although still at school, Robert worked in one of the three souvenir shops selling the club's mementoes. His shop was tiny, 6 x 5 feet, and he would have maybe twenty people queuing outside prior to the game. He had a till drawer to put cash in, and Pat Charlton (his boss) was lovely. He mainly sold football programmes, and past editions sold well too. Other inexpensive articles included rosettes and scarves. People did not buy all the expensive football clothing available for purchase nowadays.

After closing the shop, he would have a minute to dash round the corner to get into Ayresome Park football ground and dash back to the shop again, once the match was over, to reopen.

Back in those days, the young trainee football players were housed in digs. Usually, an ordinary three or four bedded property, nothing posh, with the

professionals living in normal houses locally. Robert recalls the manager, Jack Charlton, arriving in a posh Range Rover type of vehicle to the training grounds and watching the players practising in thunder and lightning from the top stands. During this period, the coal miner's strikes in 1973 and 1974 were on. No floodlights were allowed, so games were played earlier in the afternoon. The local people still found a shilling to spend to go in the *bob end* of the grounds, which was the equivalent to a new five pence.

The residential areas around the ground were manic on match days. The grounds had a capacity of 34,000 – imagine all those supporters trying to park and queue for home games. At halftime, pretty young women would parade the pitch's football score, and other leagues' scores were put up on cards around the grounds. Robert was also a member of the supporter's club, which he said felt like *family*, along with the ground staff.

There were 10-15 coaches leaving Middlesbrough and Stockton to take supporters to the away games. After agreeing to look after the number 3 bus, Robert found himself selling ham and egg buns to the punters. Robert loved the away games with his bus – sometimes setting off at midnight – a full 24 hours of buzz and entertainment.

My boyfriend, David, drove to one away game at Burnley in December 1975, only having to go to Burnley hospital to have his head stitched after having a brick thrown at him. After also having a tetanus injection, he drove home but didn't let on to his mam. Four days later, after having his stitches removed at work, his mam found out and was not best pleased.

During the summer breaks, Robert would be employed painting the seats and sweeping and cleaning up. He wore old crimplene trousers and remembered his legs being black from the dust and muck when he returned to his nana's house for lunch. Nana was employed serving drinks to the press, whereas his mam, Sally, cleaned and served basic food like sausage rolls to the directors at halftime. The ground staff were also a friendly bunch, getting the same bus and tickets together. They all knew each other and met socially at the Marton Country Club. This was a big part of Robert's growing up era and was a good excuse to drink half a pint of beer.

A few years before, we used to meet up with some of the Boro players like David Armstrong, Tony MacAndrew, Craggs and a couple of others, with Dad keeping his beady eye on them. Interestingly, Tony MacAndrew was the youngest player on the squad to score a hat-trick for the Boro back then, after scoring against Sheffield United. This record still stands today. He had a nasty streak and played that way too. His career led him to become a youth coach, having no regrets, yet recognising he owes everything to his time at the Boro.

Gillian's Wedding

Robert recalls Middlesbrough riding high in 1973/1974 after Jack Charlton arrived as manager. Four straight wins set the promotion bandwagon rolling, guaranteeing to finish as Second Division champions. This brightened up the town and had a massive influence on people's emotions during the dark days of the strikes.

Sadly, if the Boro team loses, the supporters' world can be shattered. The enjoyment can shift. People can somehow elevate football to a god-like status, with more care for the team's advancement and performance than putting football in its rightful place. Not a god-thing to be worshipped but a good thing to be enjoyed.

A few years later, Robert met the real love of his life, my sister Ann. She first

Ann's Wedding

Gillian's Wedding

'saw' this suave, grown-up young man when he called to collect Francy to take her to her boyfriend's house party. It turned out Robert and Dave Hindson were friends. He was wearing a cream jacket and aviator glasses, and Ann decided she was quite partial to blondes. Months later, at The Top Deck nightclub in Redcar, their paths crossed again when Dave Hindson and Robert asked them to dance. Ann recalls them getting on well and him asking her if he could buy her a drink.

He nearly fell over when he found a Tequila Sunrise would set him back 50p. Back then, a drink used to last us all evening – it could be left unattended and remain untouched whenever we went back to it. Robert had a £5 note in his pocket, which would usually cover an evening out as well as a taxi home. Arriving home in the early hours had Robert asking Ann out on a date.

Ann's Wedding

The rest is history, with them marrying on 23rd December 1978. They too went to see Father Crowley, who gave them permission to marry, as Robert was baptised into the Church of England. Robert attended the following three masses when the banns were read. The following week, Father Crowley preached that anyone who wasn't a Roman Catholic was not good enough to marry.

Dad put his hand in his pocket, giving this young couple £150 towards the cost of their wedding. Robert's grandmother made Ann's wedding dress. Bridesmaid's dresses were borrowed (from Gilly's wedding the previous February), Uncle Les took the photos, and the church was already decorated with flowers as it was Christmastime. Robert's parents contributed to the wedding breakfast in Acklam, bought their cake and paid for taxis. Yet, despite the budget, they had a fabulous day that set them up for a long and happy marriage.

Prior to Ann's marriage, I still attended Mass at Sacred Heart Church on Sunday mornings. Whilst singing in the choir loft, I noticed the altar at the far end of the church looked blurred.

Mam recorded:

"Rosie is having a bit of trouble with her eyes; they are very bloodshot. She got some eye drops from the chemist."

The problem with my eyes didn't clear up, and after a visit to see Dr Strachan, I was sent to get my eyes tested at the opticians. I was suffering from myopia R7L and was prescribed spectacles. Keeping Dad up to date, she wrote:

"Rosie has been busy this week. She had a couple of fillings at the dentists, and one day she walked in with her new glasses on. I didn't even recognise her! They looked like two soup plates. Everyone says how smart they are. They should be for that price!"

A major milestone in Francy's life was leaving home at the age of nineteen. She no longer wanted to live under the watchful eye of our parents and found a flat in a place called Eston, on the outskirts of Middlesbrough. Not an easy decision. She learned many life lessons on responsibility, including paying bills from her Yorkshire Bank account and taking care of herself.

Thankfully, the Civil Service housed canteens in all places of work. People took advantage of these hearty subsidized meals, along with the canteen trolleys that arrived at our desks each day. These were laden with scones, pastries and all sorts of other delicious treats. Francy made the most of these opportunities to eat homemade type food. It saved her money that could be spent enjoying herself at the weekend.

The three of us were healthy eaters and looked young for our age. People would tease me and say I would be fat at 40 years of age because of what I could tuck away.

Gilly was about to face a significant event in her life too. At nineteen, she had asked Mam to allow her to get engaged to Neil. Mam refused. Gilly continued to see Neil, often watching him play football matches and then going to the pub after. Coming in late at night was causing arguments with Mam, and in June 1976, she wrote to Dad:

"Things are very quiet at home, except I have been having another talk with Gillian about being out every night for the last week and coming home late. As usual, this has ended up in a crying match with this story about nobody liking Neil, and he wasn't welcome in our house. I'm going to see if Gill starts coming in any earlier next week and if she has taken any notice of our talk."

This was the last airmail letter to be written as Dad returned home in early July. One evening, another argument broke out with Dad accusing Gilly of treating the home like a hotel. I remember going in the hall and seeing the situation escalate with Gilly storming out to the Sullivan's. Dad sent me to go and get her back, but she struggled to cope with the rules of the house like Francy. Her suitcase was packed, and she left home under a cloud of her parents' disapproval of the man she was to marry. After living with Neil's parents for a few weeks, she lived with his Aunty Eleanor in Middlesbrough town centre. It was like going back in time. Her new *home* was a two up and two down town house with no bathroom. Not even a tin bath. A quick *lick and a promise* through the week, which alludes to washing performed by children. Then on a weekend, Gilly filled up the washing up bowl, stepped in and started from her head down and had a more complete clean. Aunty Eleanor had a modern outlook and was happy that Gilly was engaged to her nephew. She treated her as a daughter and allowed my sister to live the life of a nineteen-year-old. Both women respected each other despite the age difference and hardship. Then came a *great move* from town to the suburb of Hemlington, situated on the edge of Middlesbrough. Gilly was still living with Eleanor and helped with the move to a lovely bright open flat on the second floor of this new community building. She remembers a big picture window, but the best thing was opening the door to the bathroom with central heating. Both commenting, "Like luxury, living here."

Aunty Eleanor fed Gilly some strange delights, and one of her favourites was tinned chicken supreme on toast. She was not a cook. Employed in the dairy, bottling milk, this lady also had a compassionate and caring side to her nature. Her strong Catholic beliefs had her faith taking her on several trips to Lourdes. My sister said Eleanor was a *real Godsend*.

Although in employment with the Civil Service, Gilly wanted to do additional work to save for her wedding. It was her future mother-in-law who suggested working in the pub, helping her and Danny. Now happily engaged, all their spare cash was placed into a savings account. Neil worked extra shifts to add to this, and soon about £3000 was raised. Added to this was interest on this amount and, to Gilly, this was amazing as it was like getting free money. In the following December of 1977, they bought their first property in Acklam. Much like my sister Ann, this spurred them to bring the wedding day forward to February 1978, much to Mam and Dad's disapproval. Gilly was happy when the wedding was over, mainly because she hated being the centre of attention and was like Francy in that respect.

Francy also left home and, with Ann marrying in the December, I was the only daughter left in our family house to begin the New Year of 1979.

Suddenly, after nearly twenty years of living together in our family home, growing up brought the catalyst for change. There was major disruption within the Farrow family, and Mam must have suffered with *empty nest syndrome*, grieving as the primary carer of her offspring.

Although two of her daughters had left under a cloud, it was only a few years later that the dust had settled, and family ties were once more re-established. Did I think more about my relationship with my triplet sisters than with God? Personally, the answer would be a yes, but for Francy, this was definitely a no. Some people might think this love we had for each other was a form of *worship*. The truth is that the close unconditional love we had, helped us have the capacity to love and accept others in a similar way, creating depth in our friendships and not just forming casual acquaintances, like our Dad did. He had a wide circle of friends but only a slight knowledge of who these people were.

However, this close, tightly-knit triplet relationship began to change as we all embarked on close relationships with the husbands and partners in our lives. Being a triplet was such fun. After our early years of taking our first steps together, speaking as one and having Saturday jobs together, we became individuals. We were even poorly together as children, and I hold a recently found postcard given to me by Uncle Alan. This postcard is dated 10th August

1960, and Grandad Leo's sister wrote to their mam, stating:

"Dear Mum and Auntie Edie,
Hope all are well. Have had a sunny journey so far.
Just having tea in Welshpool.
Leo is still at Rene's; they have tonsillitis and he is looking after them.
Love to all, Henry and Win xx."

This postcard is amazing as it answers my question of how often Grandad came to visit Mam in Coventry when we were babies. We would have been just over three years of age when he arrived to help with our care. We would have had a fever, sore

Front and back of Postcard sent from Welshpool in 1960

throats, trouble swallowing, with symptoms lasting weeks. No wonder Mam needed her father's help. Proof he did visit.

Gilly, especially, continued to suffer from tonsillitis growing up, and Francy always had ear infections. Both, as teenagers, were troubled with sore throats, runny noses and headaches. Francy recalls always being poorly for three days from pain relief after the dentist's fillings. She just thought everyone felt the same way. Both ended up at the doctor, and their problems were flagged up as needing medical attention. Both had allergies to either the preservatives in cocaine-based injections or dairy-based foods. Francy would later be discovered as having the same intolerance as Gilly. Appointments were made to see the specialist at The North Riding Infirmary on Newport Road. This served as an ear, nose and throat hospital, treating generations of Teessiders and their families until closure in 2003.

Interestingly, both my sisters have different memories of how the medical procedures came about and what took place. Francy recalls going to the hospital to have her sinuses washed out and the lining removed from her nasal cavities.

A discovery was made of a bony growth in her nose. After the operation, big cotton buds with cocaine-based medication were placed up her nose to ease the bleeding. Asked by the nurse how she was feeling, Francy told her she had pins and needles up her arms and legs and felt funny. The nurse told her she would talk to the consultant who had done the operation and returned with a wheelchair. She was immediately placed in a hospital bed and got a telling off for not letting people know that she was allergic to the medication. She explained she didn't think she was. Her blood pressure had lowered due to the unusual reaction from the procedure. She was kept in for observation in case she started to have convulsions. The handsome doctor had a strange effect on her blood pressure, causing it to rise. In the end, we shouted for the nurse to come and see her.

On the other hand, Gilly recalls that she and her sister had bony growths on opposite sides of their noses. However, the staff were aware of Gilly's previous reaction to the epidural. The problem of her intolerance to cocaine-based medication was highlighted to the staff.

I recall visiting them both in hospital and being extremely worried and concerned after seeing blood-stained clothes and buds up their noses. The medical team were very interested in meeting the third triplet. They asked me to have the same operation as my siblings. The answer was a quick, "No, thank you". I had taken Francy a box of Maltesers, but she felt too ill to eat any. I opened the box and demolished the lot, something she has never forgotten. Francy recovered well but still was affected by eating dairy products. Her overall health did improve, though.

Gilly continued to suffer side effects from tonsillitis. Each bout lasting three weeks and requiring her to be on the sick from work. The situation got so bad, she was afraid she would lose her job. So, at the age of thirty-one, she had her tonsils removed, helping her recover to better health.

Clearly, we were still very close and drew strength from being and spending time together. We were not jealous of each other and didn't feel quite whole without the other two around.

Interestingly, recalling these memories brought to mind how Ann might have felt about being the younger sister to her older three triplet sisters? I have read accounts that having triplet sisters left people feeling like only children and that they seemed like strangers. Thankfully, Ann's experiences were not like this at all. She didn't feel the odd one out and was especially close to the youngest triplet, Gilly. I think it helped that we were all girls and quite close in age. She states that it was, "Water off a duck's back to me, being bossed about by you lot back then." The airmail letters hold testimony to this truth, with us all informing Dad about our social life.

Ann wrote:

"Enough of college, do you know? Of course not! That Francy and I are going to the swimming baths on Friday. I've had butterflies in my tummy since I knew. We are going with my Dave and her Dave. She didn't want to go without me. I am borrowing Gill's bikini, it's very nice, and the girls say it looks nice on."

Francy wrote:

"Snug and I are going to the baths with the two Dave's. Confess I am nervous but am determined to learn to swim properly."

Interestingly, they hadn't been swimming since third year at the convent. Ann got her breadth certificate, and even that took some doing. Mam laughingly told them she was going to phone Middlesbrough Baths to warn them.

I wrote:

"Guess what? Thomas would like to take Snug out. I don't think she minds either. I'll keep an eye on them for you."

Gilly wrote:

"You know the pictures we had taken on holiday? Well, we had them developed. Great, they are, and I think the scenes are really good, considering daft Fran and Snug took them! Everybody at home is quite happy and we are all getting on well."

Mam wrote:

"All the girls and Julie took Bernie Glynn to the Top Deck, and they all had a nice time. Ann had a free day from college this week. We ended up at Scarborough on a beeline trip. I find I get tired after I've been walking about and kept falling asleep on the bus. Ann kept waking me up because she thought I would start snoring."

At the end of the day, Ann didn't have a choice or say about being born as our younger sister. I think Mam made a conscious effort to include Ann in conversations and life, with me sometimes concluding that Ann was her favourite. I think, deep down, I have a hidden worry that our younger sister had drawn the short straw. But maybe not, as Ann states:

"One baby as compared to three – things must have been sooo much easier for Mam second time round, and you three will understand that more than me! So, that and no enforced separation may well be the primary causes of any difference in my bond with Mam compared to yours. Also, second children are usually pretty laid back which may well have suited Mam's character. So, her favourite, maybe."

The enforced stay in Nazareth House, when us triplets were between four to five years of age, will have indeed severed bonds with our parents, no longer giving up a secure attachment to them. But thankfully, we had an inseparable closeness with one another. We clearly loved Mam, showering her with gifts and that Christmas of 1975, she writes to Dad saying:

"The girls gave me some beautiful cards with little animals on them. Rosie and Francy gave me a lovely cardigan, Snug gave me a red leather purse and Gill, a Roger Whitaker record. I have boxes of chocolates – they all seem to be Black Magic. Everyone seemed so kind, going out of their way to make sure I wasn't lonely."

Looking back, I may have struggled to honour my mother and father for decisions made during our childhood, but things are always more complex than they appear. After the passage of time, my perspective on them both has changed. With the gift of hindsight, I can reflect on the lessons that enable me to have 20/20 vision on both the successes and failures in our upbringing. Grateful that these experiences have provided the starting point and scaffolding of what is written in this book.

Chapter Five – The way it was

The way it was back then, wives were seen but not heard. Our Mam belonged to the silent generation – born between 1925-1945 and was brought up during war time in an economic depression. There was real inequality between her expected role in life, compared to her husband's. Mam was expected to remain in the home as a housewife and care for her four daughters, whilst Dad worked, often travelling abroad for long periods. Mam was left with all the chores and disciplining teenagers, which would have no doubt been much easier with him around.

Francy, Gilly & Rosie – Teenagers

As young girls, Dad only had to look at us sternly, and we would burst out crying. Even as teenagers, we were wary and sometimes scared of him. Mam was highly intelligent, having benefitted from her education at the Newlands Convent, but Dad, however, only had a school certificate in Mathematics and English and went to Dorman Long Co. Ltd as an apprentice electrician.

So, after working for seven years as a clerk at Peckston's (the local shipping office), Mam's life was soon to change, giving birth to triplet baby girls. Stepping into a world of silence and unable to share this burden with close family or friends, her life in Coventry became even more silent. There is a saying, *sent to Coventry*, which means being ignored or ostracised. The landlady of the property Dad and Mam rented told them in no uncertain terms that they would have to move out after our birth. Even Mam's best friend, Aunty Cecelia, was thrust into the same world of drudgery after having her children. I wonder how often they would think, "What could have been?".

There were so many babies born during that time, with the contraceptive pill still to be invented. The pill was introduced in 1961 and was available on the National Health Service.

However, you could only get this from your GP if you were married and with your husband's consent. This did not change until 1967. Back then, couples got married, *then* lived together. They were a hardy bunch, and when you think of how the world has changed from my mam's era to nowadays, no wonder they are confused, and there is a generation gap.

Around 1975, I went with my sister, Gilly, to see Dr Strachen to discuss whether or not he would prescribe the pill for her. We knew that family planning clinics were prescribing single women this tiny pill, a controversial decision at the time. People had questions like, "Should a young woman's parents be told?". The pill changed the dynamics in relationships. Women said they felt pressured into taking this contraceptive pill. Others may be citing the problem of heavy periods (as the pill can make periods more regular) as the reason for their appointment or justification for taking it. In 1975, Loretta Lynn recorded a country music song titled, *The Pill*. Rural physicians highlighted how this song had brought more success to the rural areas than all the literature they had generally made available to the public. As young, engaged women, we thought it was in our best interest to protect against any unwanted pregnancies. This was liberating for women, as with its introduction, women had control over when they wanted to have a family – a lifestyle choice that women were trusted to make.

This was also the decade of long, soft, big hairstyles, and now employed, we could afford to go to a *proper* hairdresser. Previous to this, Francy has a vague memory of me getting my hair cut shorter at the hairdressers on Cumberland Road. With rats' tails dangling down the back of my neck, her and Gilly quickly following suit. When we were younger, Francy considered it a labour of love to be my personal

Gillian & Frances – More like twins

hairdresser. I was often seen with my hair in plaits, a ponytail, bunches or a bun – I never liked my hair down, tickling my face. I really liked my hair shorter and, much to my parent's dismay, I made a further appointment at Cameo's on Linthorpe Road. Sitting in the chair, I asked for a *pixie* cut. Carol, the stylist, proceeded to give me the shortest haircut in the world. As I watched the rats' tails drop to the floor, I felt disappointed, and that night, I cried myself to sleep, thinking that I had made the wrong decision. But that all fell away the next morning as I looked in the mirror, and I loved my new hairstyle. Over the following months, women stopped me in the town to ask where I had been to get my hair cut and what the style was called.

Another popular hair-do was the *stack perm*. Mam was often seen sporting small tight curls after her trip to Cameo's. If the perm didn't take and her curls quickly dropped out, she would be straight back on the phone asking for it to be done again.

Ann, my younger sister, remembers going with her friend Sharon to an Italian hairdresser closer to the town. The guy was flamboyant and had them both stand in the middle of the salon while he asked them if they both really wanted a fringe. With the answer being, "Yes", he cut their fringes there and then. It was the first time Ann had had her hair washed in one of those *special sinks*. The salon may have been Guido's – this hairdresser opened in 1961 in Russell Street, the first

Marion in curlers

of its kind in Middlesbrough. My mother-in-law, Marion, also permed her hair. However, this was done at home with her girlfriends, which was probably a lot cheaper. I can imagine the fun and laughter as these ladies tried to copy the stack perm. Lots of perm rods were stacked away from the head on things like chopsticks, only perming the middle and lower parts of their long hair. The crown area was left untouched, creating a halo of curls. This process resulted in tight curls to bubble-like creations.

Around this period, I was invited to David's family home to meet his parents and two sisters. Helen, his younger sister by ten years, remembers me going to Sunday tea and being amazed at the spread of food on the table. Her mam always liked to impress and loved baking cakes, scones and flapjacks. Now and then, I would be invited around after work for dinner. Helen knew I worked at the tax office and thought it sounded really important, recalling me looking very smart in tight pencil skirts and blouses and wearing high heels. Apparently, I told her that my sisters and I shared clothes. If I bought something new, I wore it first and then put it in a shared wardrobe.

My first experience of Christmas tradition in the Gott household was a pile of homemade Yorkshire puddings being put on my plate with lots of gravy. To my surprise, these were to be eaten *before* the Christmas dinner. Very strange, but so tasty. This was followed by the customary Christmas lunch, with David having second helpings of this delicious food placed in front of him. Next came the Christmas pudding, which was set alight after having a ladleful of brandy carefully poured over it. After the flames had died down, it was then served with a brandy sauce. A couple of hours later, a slice of Marion's Christmas cake, with a wedge of Wensleydale cheese, would complete the afternoon of festivities. By home time, I felt like the proverbial turkey – stuffed. The Christmas of 1975 was very different in the Farrow household. Dad was working abroad in Bahrain, and consequently, this was our first ever Christmas without him home to join in the fun. Mam had written to Dad on the 20th and 23rd of December, she had posted him a parcel on the 10th and:

Someone in Francie's office told her there was a strike in Saudi Arabia, and at the Post Office she had been told there was a go-slow over there."

The money Mam needed to buy coats for our gifts had been brought round by a man called Bill Richardson.

He also promised to arrange a further Christmas advance for her – no doubt he was one of Dad's bosses. The air mail letter dated the 23rd said:

"Gill found herself a lovely coat."

This was later described by Gilly:

"Plum with other colours running through it. It's heavy and very smart with a wide skirt, and it doesn't half look posh."

Clearly, Mam didn't like the one I chose:

"Rosie went dotty over this coat she saw in a window. Luckily it was a small size. It is made of chenille and reminds me of those horrible tablecloths and curtains that were the fashion years ago."

Writing to Dad on 9/1/76, I told him how much I loved my gift:

"I got a smashing Christmas present off you and Mam, a lovely rust coat – it buttons nearly all the way down the front and like Gill's, it has a flared skirt and a belt. I got two nighties, a pair of slippers, a flea (made of stone) – Mam calls it my brain! Christmas was full of excitement (as it usually is), but it wasn't the same without you there to clown around. I miss you, as does everyone else."

The same month, Gilly wrote asking Dad:

"What type of Christmas did you have, and did you like your pressies? Boy I didn't half miss you. No Dad to see open his presents and that's most the fun, isn't it? Seeing the expressions on their faces. Do you know we made Mam open her pressies as soon as we gave her them? Hope you didn't cheat and open yours too early."

These air mail letters captured the everyday events during Dad's employment abroad and thankfully have been capturing, in fine detail, the music of this era too. Several references are as follows:

"I've bought a new record, Art Garfunkel's 'Breakaway' and 'My Little Town'. Both are famous hits. I've also been playing some of your records, mostly Sinatra and The Beatles (hope you don't mind). Rosie."

Ann wrote:

"At the moment I am listening to The Osmond's on the record player, which is a Christmas present from you and Mam. It's a lovely record."

My special memories and gifts from David were the popular records of that decade – *Dancing Queen* by Abba and *Band of Gold* recorded by Freda Payne. Strangely enough, Mam's favourite was *Ride A White Swan* by T-Rex. This was written by Mark Bolan, who suggested he wrote the song after he was spiked with LSD at the launch of the British version of The Rolling Stones magazine. This monthly magazine focuses on music, politics and popular culture. I always thought the song had strange lyrics. This song was also liked by my cousin, Anthony. When he hears *Dreamer* by Supertramp, it invariably transports him back to the No. 1 Radio School at RAF Locking. Supertramp was an English rock band producing progressive rock sounds. However, if you are looking for sunshiny music, the 1970s have it – for me personally, it was the happiest decade. The pop music was so upbeat, and in 1973 John Denver sang, "Sunshine on my shoulders makes me happy". These were lyrics I could understand and relate to:

"If I had a wish that I could wish for you
I'd make a wish for sunshine all the while
Sunshine almost always makes me high."

No need for any drug-taking to produce this beautiful sound.

Both our really close friends lived near Nazareth House, and we would all visit each other's homes. Bernie fondly recalls dancing to Top of the Pops in our front room and going nightclubbing to the Madison in town with us. Julie remembers staying at our house quite a bit. Our mam and dad were always so welcoming, especially us having a New Year's Eve party at Hereford Close. Pop charts would sound around the house from the radio playing the official singles countdown to the top ten:

10. Happy to be on an Island in the Sun — Demis Roussos
9. Itchy Coo Park — The Small Faces
8. King of the Cops — Billy Howard
7. Wide Eyes and Legless — Andy Fairweather–Low
6. Let's Twist Again — Chubby Checker
5. Art for Art's Sake — 10CC
4. In Dulci Jubilo — Mike Oldfield
3. Mamma Mia — Abba
2. Glass of Champagne — Sailor
1. Bohemian Rhapsody — Queen

However, back in the late 1940s, rock music was Grandmother's lullaby, Eldrado was an ice cream, a gay person was the life and soul of the party and nothing more, while aids just meant beauty treatment or help for someone in trouble. These survivors were born before television, before penicillin, polio shots, and they had never heard of FM radio. This generation found joy in the simple things of life. The Second World War had ended, and it was time to enjoy life to the full, especially as children. Normal life for them had been going into Auntie's air-raid shelter, or ones down the road, though they never played in them. Bombs had dropped close by, but fires were quickly put out. Brave relatives were involved in the resistance, some being police and soldiers. But as children during this time, they never worried like their parents did. The end of the war made for happy days, playing outside in the streets with skipping ropes, marbles, tip-tap and swinging round the lamp posts.

Happy, but without luxuries, everything was a treat in those days. Trips to the park, even the pictures three times a week, if you were lucky. An older friend, Beryl, remembers a friend getting a packet of sweets from America when they came off rationing. Her eyes nearly popped out of her head seeing these jelly sweets. After picking a ginger one to eat, Beryl was poorly for days with an upset tummy. Her father would give his children his sweet ration on the one condition – they didn't choose chewing gum. They never did. People were happy to buy sliced bread and slabs of butter, and the children would get liquorice, which they were told was good for their teeth. No need to go to the dentist eating healthy homemade meals each evening. Biscuits were loose and scooped into a bag, cakes were baked – big Christmas cakes with no waste. If women didn't use their rations, they were pooled together to make baked treats for the staff and patients on the hospital wards.

Before the National Health Service days in 1948, operations and trips to the doctor or dentist had to be paid for. Consequently, it was usually a serious problem that warranted health care. Beryl, as a child, spent time in hospital with her parents paying for her care that was totted up on the back of the rent book. Some people suffered long and hard.

Medicine boxes in the family home would hold:

- Vaseline for dry and sensitive skin
- Germolene cream for sore knees and used as an antiseptic
- Witch Hazel used for sore throats and nappy rash
- Oil of Juniper used for toothache
- Milk of Magnesia for tummy ache
- Cuticura for bites and stings

Other friends, Celia and Carol, recall their mam giving them cod liver oil, rose hip syrup, Scott's emulsion, malt and a bile bean (taken on a Friday evening). Scott's emulsion was thought to be the Holy Grail of supplements. It was an excellent product, helping to prevent colds and flu and helped develop bones and teeth.

A poem has been penned, called *Cornwall In Childhood:*

"Come, Hygiene, goddess of the growing boy,
I here salute thee in Sanatogen!
Anaemic girls need Virol, but for me
Be Scott's Emulsion, rusks and Mellin's Food,
Cod-liver oil and malt, and for my neck
Wright's Coal tar soap, Euthymol for my teeth."

Beryl recalls her mother making everything from scratch. Food was made from raw or base ingredients; sheets were even mended in exchange for half-pound of margarine. Doll's heads were bought, bodies assembled with the help of being stuffed with old tights. Crimping scissors were used to produce post office sets and stamps. Women would go to the market or Binns on remnant day to buy odds and ends of material and wool. With mothers sometimes making their daughter's clothing until they got married. These talented ladies continued to make their grandchildren's clothes, even having the gift, expertise, and skill to produce wedding dresses. As money began to come in after the war, households needed to replace household goods and belongings, even saving

every week for an annual holiday. This generation existed before househusbands, computer dating, dual careers, and a 'meaningful relationship' meant getting along with cousins, while sheltered accommodation was where you waited for a bus.

Past memories came flooding back for these three ladies of goods sold from the back of vans. These goods varied from carpets, lavender polish, fish, bread and Ringtons tea. They even recall the vegetable man arriving at 11pm, tooting his horn to let his customers know he'd arrived. By far, the favourite was the Lowcocks Lemonade lorries.

They had regular buyers and would knock on people's doors. This drink was top of the pops and holds a special place in the hearts of the North East drinkers. Flavours like dandelion and burdock, and cream soda were amongst the favourites. The name Lowcocks has been around in Middlesbrough for decades. With their famous quart bottle being so well made, it was a popular replacement for a hot water bottle. I remember as a child, Dad filling it with hot water at bedtime. Over the years, it became easier to have these drinks delivered each day via the milkman.

When a severe flu epidemic hit the town in 1957, the Lowcocks factory worked flat out as hot lemonade was regarded as a remedy for the flu. Writing this brought back childhood memories of a Lowcocks ice cream soda, fizzling with a dollop of ice cream, sat in our back garden of Hereford Close. A forward-thinking company that encouraged recycling, giving a tenpence refund on a returned bottle, sadly is now consigned to history.

Sometimes life-changing events can overlap generations. One such event was the birth of the National Health Service in July 1948. Like the ICI works at Billingham, this was a cradle to the grave organisation, believing good healthcare should be available to everyone. Patients were to come first. The NHS was there to improve our health and well-being. To get us better when we are ill and help us stay as well as possible to the end of our lives. For the first time, dentists, hospitals, nurses, pharmacists and doctors were brought together, free for all to access help and care in their time of need. The NHS planned not to just treat illness but to promote good health. Introducing revolutionary scans like the CT scan and MRI scan, which provides detailed images of the inside of people's bodies. In the 1980s, keyhole surgery was also made available to remove the gallbladder with an optic cable.

Fifty per cent of antibiotics were discovered during 1950-1960, and this period is called the *golden age of discovery*. Diseases that previously killed people, like bacterial pneumonia, increased survival rates of patients when treated with this medication. We were a generation brought up on penicillin in the era of widely available antibiotics. Gillian was often at the doctor's and was very susceptible to bouts of tonsillitis and was often prescribed bottles of medicine to fight off these infections, to be taken for 7-14 days. Nowadays, antibiotic resistance is a big problem due to being over prescribed in the past. Taking antibiotics when you don't need them can mean they will not work for you in the future. They are no longer used for viral infections nor for ear infections or chest infections in children. People are encouraged to let minor illnesses resolve on their own without medication. Thus, preventing the development of antibiotic resistance. It is known that prolonged use can have side effects leading to tooth decay, yeast infections, mouth sores, asthma, allergics, stomach upsets, and may be related to obesity and diabetes.

Interestingly, I have found an article about the Stepney triplets born in shattered, post-war Britain. Margaret, Barry and Stephen were born in 1951 and *no one was allowed to breathe on us.*

With no IVF, multiple births were a rare occurrence and triplets were hardly ever seen. Born into a bleak, grey, east-end life for millions of new mams was one of

Stepney Triplets

bone-numbing hard work. Life was one long chilly slog due to the freezing winters, power cuts and coal shortages. The triplets' mother, Amy, took pride in her family being well turned out. She had her hands full constantly, but she was utterly selfless and surrounded them with love. The full article is written up in the Daily Express in the edition dated 4/1/2020. It was fascinating to read, giving me an insight into our own mam's struggles with daily life. Also in this article was a picture of a letter from the Privy Purse Office at Buckingham Palace, with Mrs Amy Oakes receiving a cheque for three pounds, with His Majesty's good wishes for the children's future welfare. This gladdened my heart to

see this, as our letter from Her Majesty the Queen went missing after we Farrow triplets were born.

I hold the original envelope, dated 7th October 1957, with the Privy Purse stamp, but the actual letter was lost in the post. After reading this account, I have decided

that maybe Mam's life was less traumatic than Mrs Oakes'. Hopefully, we too were rays of sunshine that drew others to our Silver Cross pram. Clearly, people were touched with Mam's plight, stuffing money under the pram covers to help with our care – the kindness of strangers.

We know from our mam that she didn't venture out much with the three of us. I always thought the reason was that it

The proud parents

took two hours to prepare for this type of adventure. Or maybe, like Amy Oakes, she didn't want other children or adults touching or breathing over us due to the outbreak of Polio and the Asian Flu in Coventry in 1957.

We Farrow triplets were born in Coventry and lived in Willenhall, a suburb of this city. It was initially a small village until it was incorporated into Coventry and expanded after the Second World War, with the building of many council houses. We lived on the St James estate in a council home: 28 Mary Stessor Street.

Just two days before our arrival into the world, the Minister of Health announced an increase in vaccine production to fight against Polio. A devastating outbreak in Coventry affected more than a hundred people, just as the city was being redeveloped and a vaccine was becoming available. Some patients who

Stepney triplets as adults

caught this virus would be left paralysed and unable to breathe without the help of *an iron lung*. The lung was like a large coffin and very frightening, but it proved to be a life saver for so many. The British vaccine continued to be administered throughout the summer of 1957 for children below ten years of age. There was hope at that time being voiced that the world would be Polio-free within a few years. Yet, it would not be until the 1980s that this would be so in the UK. People live with the after-effects of this preventable disease. The United Kingdom is a leader in Polio eradication, with a recent commitment to aid in the immunisation of 45 million children worldwide. Globally, the numbers of cases are in steep decline, but more needs to be done to completely eliminate this disease.

However, in the June of 1957, the first cases of Asian Flu were reported in the United Kingdom. This virus outbreak caused a similar global disaster to Covid-19 and was first identified in East Asia. London was at the centre of the World Influenza Research and tracking of the virus. In the UK, nine million people caught the Asian Flu, and out of a population of around 51 million, 14,000 died. The following August, the virus hit schools and communities across the North West. In the October, a vaccine against this strain of influenza was produced at the Wright-Fleming Institute of Microbiology in West London. It was to be distributed free on the National Health Service. The medical priority to give the fullest protection against this flu strain was to receive two injections less than three weeks apart.

Doctors, nurses and other medical staff were given priority, taking the workload in dealing with this virus. Like Covid-19, the elderly and those with heart or lung disease are the virus' chief victims after secondary problems arise, such as bronchial pneumonia. The virus mutates easily, meaning a new vaccine must be produced to deal with each strain. It was rare for an epidemic to be transmitted beyond national boundaries and become a pandemic back then. By August 1958, the Asian Flu had run its course.

Ten years later, in 1968, the Hong Kong Flu pandemic hit the world. It was suspected that this virus strain evolved from the previous strain of influenza that caused the 1957 pandemic. Because this new virus retained the antigen N2, some people had retained immune protection against this latest strain, with far fewer deaths than the 1918-1919 outbreak. The rapid development of a vaccine against the H2N2 virus and the availability of antibiotics to treat secondary infections limited the spread and mortality of the pandemic.

No doubt, the rate at which Covid-19 spread globally is unprecedented. However, its rapid global spread will be attributed to the high rates of passenger travel characterizing our modern times.

It appears those born before June 1940 were a hardy bunch. Where *made in Japan* meant shoddy workmanship, the term *making out* referred to how you did in your exams, *a stud* was something that fastened your collar to your shirt and *going all the way* meant staying on the double-decker to the bus depot.

My friends, Celia, Carol and Beryl, are indeed a hardy bunch, capable of enduring the difficulties, hardships and adverse conditions that life threw at them. A generation who has counted its blessings and provided a gift of social history from their generation to ours.

Chapter Six – Work

L ife in the 1970s was a time of feast or famine within the workplace, alternating between shortage or an overabundance of money within many people's home situations. This was the decade of strikes. The miners went on strike in 1972 after wage negotiations collapsed, causing a three-day week to be introduced to save on electricity. Some people couldn't afford to turn the heating on at all. Others recall the streets being cloaked in darkness and that being out and about at this time was scary. This state of emergency ended after seven weeks. Britain suffered a long period of frequent strikes, severe inflation with rising unemployment during this decade.

My husband, David, was 18 years old in 1973 and remembers getting petrol

Frank Farrow (Dad) Triplets!

vouchers for his motorbike. He was travelling to Billingham ICI and completing his four-year apprenticeship as a pipe fitter.

Us triplets were fifteen years old in 1972 and had started work at Jaffa's, 152-154 Gilkes Street in Middlesbrough. The three of us took turns to work each Saturday, and if it was busy, the owners had the other two triplets to call on. Job sharing even before it became a modern term. Jaffa's shop was a haberdashery selling small items like buttons, zips, thread, lace and ribbons. The premises were stuffed full of paraphernalia necessary for every sewing activity, held in glass units under the counters. The rolls of fabrics were on show on shelving behind the counter. Gloves could be purchased alongside ladies' underwear. I remember giggling at the sizes of the *big ladies* knickers.

Francy recalls baby clothing too.

From researching a Jewish website, I discovered that the Jaffa family were residents in Middlesbrough from the 1890s until the 1970s. Records reveal that on the 11th of January 1950, Eric Jaffa married Patricia Vera Cowan at the Park Road South Synagogue. He was in employment as a master tailor, and she was a tailor's clerk. Their home addresses were given as 351 Linthorpe Road and 30 Oxford Road in Middlesbrough. These details prove the existence of the shop on Gilkes Street, where we worked. I remember Mrs Jaffa having jet black hair and sallow skin. She must have been very kind and patient with her three assistants, maybe wondering why she had to repeat numerous instructions to the three Miss Farrows.

Diagonally opposite Jaffa's haberdashery stood Gilkes Street Swimming Baths. So, after a hard week's work in the shop, Eric Jaffa would go to the grand-sounding Turkish Baths housed within this building. He was a regular. Along with thousands of other children in the area, we learnt to swim in the Middlesbrough pool. Little realising that this Victorian, red-bricked building was a place for grown-ups to use as well.

Swimming Experiences:

Gilly remembers being pushed into the swimming pool as a young girl and always telling Dad that she had a cold when she was actually on her period. She learnt to swim at work age.

Francy mainly remembers going to the swimming baths with boyfriends when she was in her teens.

I remember being much younger and going with either school or with Dad. There were floats that you could use, flat plastic shapes, and the instructor on the side holding a long pole to rescue you if you sank or dunk you with if you were misbehaving. I also remember watching young people jumping in the pool with pyjamas on and having to collect a rubber brick from the bottom of the water. Then, to complete their bid for a certificate, jump back in to rescue a drowning person.

The changing rooms were cold and tiled, causing you to dry and quickly put your clothes back on. Hairdryers were introduced at a much later date.

At fifteen years of age, Julie recalls, "People came for a proper bath." You could have a good, hot, soak in the bath that had fancy *claw feet*. She worked there back in the day, enjoying the variety of jobs – setting up the steam room, sauna, baths and pool, ready for the public to use. If people didn't have a towel, they could hire one. Julie also did the laundry but said going through the laundry and boiler room scared her as it was said to be haunted.

She would sit with the staff and have breakfast and dinner around the pool and remembers she really enjoyed her years working there, as she loved sports. Memories close to her heart are being told the stories of Jack Hatfield practising swimming when the pool was empty. He was allowed to do this as his dad was a superintendent there. This young man went on to represent Great Britain in the Olympics. It is written that he also trained in the River Tees, a flooded quarry in Great Ayton and in the boating lake in Albert Park, often with many hundreds of people watching him. In addition, the police came to do life-saving courses as well as galas involving competitions within schools.

This once proud building was one of the best places in Middlesbrough to meet up with fellow sportsmen needing to lose weight or tone up in the Turkish and Russian baths, the slipper baths, the shampooing room and a cooling room. These baths sadly closed in the 1980s and eventually were demolished in the next decade.

After leaving the convent in the summer of 1975, we found ourselves signing on at the job centre on Grange Road in Middlesbrough town centre. Us lasses would have walked straight down Linthorpe Road, and Francy remembers our dad in tow, even though we were 18 years of age. She remembers thinking that the only jobs available to us were with the police, nursing, or government. I only remember having two choices – either Civil Service or the chicken factory. After registering at the job centre for a short period, Mam wanted our benefit money to put towards our board and lodging, kindly giving us £1 pocket money.

Over the next few weeks, letters were written applying for jobs in the local area, with the three of us sending out letters to the various departments of the Civil Service. After successful interviews, we secured employment in the Department of Health and Social Security, The Unemployment Benefit Office, and the Tax Office in Middlesbrough and began work in October. However, I had to wait two weeks after the girls got their confirmation of work and was really worried I would still be signing on. Our first pay packet was £7.50, of which Mam took £5, leaving us with £2.50, equivalent today of about £21.

Work for us all was a baptism of fire, as the lives and morals of people in the outside world suddenly opened up to us and became a reality. But even though we were shocked after our sheltered upbringing, we all had soft hearts towards these ladies dealing and coping with life's struggles, even if it was sometimes of their own making. I was always sent to the ladies' toilets to see why other women were crying or upset. After pouring their hearts out, I would give them a hankie and a hug.

Gilly remembers her first year of training in the DHSS, with people often not pulling their weight. Other staff having health issues needed additional support. Although she felt overwhelmed with the pressures (often working weekends to catch up on the backlog), she too received support and help from the more experienced staff. Through the week, she could spend up to three hours on one case, as a widow having just lost her husband needed help claiming benefits for the first time in her life.

Francy, too, was a hard worker and spent time correcting other people's mistakes. She was often found protecting the younger staff in later years, diverting clients by stepping in. She often travelled to different offices, covering and training other staff.

My job, however, was a different kettle of fish. I didn't have the pressure of dealing with the public face to face. The pressure came from answering the phones, never knowing the type of enquiry or question that was going to be asked of you. Which might sound odd to this generation with mobile phones.

London Provision 6 was housed in Rede House, 71 Corporation Road, Middlesbrough TS1 1TW. Within these offices were the people employed to deal with the income tax issues, comprising of thirty-two London boroughs at that time. The phone rang constantly, and I remember a young man who refused to answer any calls at all.

In the 1970s, most families we knew wouldn't have afforded a private phone in their home setting. Instead, we relied on the red phone box at the top of Lancaster Road, just off Linthorpe Village. Only 35% of households owned a landline. It certainly explains why my heart jumped every time the one on my desk rang, and both the girls felt the same way too at work.

I only ever remember *seeing* one of my tax clients. He was travelling through the area from London and arrived on LP6's doorstep. After speaking to one of my bosses, I was asked to walk him to Middlesbrough Baths as they had showers.

The next step in our working lives was to head off to different training centres, to take part in high-quality training programs for civil servants, learning the skills, knowledge and behaviours needed for successful performance in our new careers. We each had to take an oath of secrecy as part of allegiance before our assumption of duty. Very odd.

Preparations were made for me to travel to Newcastle, with Mam writing:

"Rosie has just received a cheque from work for £51 for her expenses when she goes to Newcastle; they have booked her in at a boarding house at Whitley Bay."

The following week, she wrote:

Rosie is all of a twitter because she is going to Newcastle on Monday. I think she is planning to pack everything except the kitchen sink in her case."

Mam's next letter to Dad says:

"Rosie got packed and away all right on her big adventures. She was quite excited about it. Frances had to get the 7:05 train this morning, but she seemed rather nervous about the whole thing "

I did feel excited about my first week away from under Mam's watching eye.

So on writing to Dad on 7th December 1975, I told him:

"I'm writing from Wynburn Guest House in Whitley Bay. Joan and Margaret are sharing my room, with Joan acting as our guide because she used to live here when she was younger. We caught the 10:40 train to Newcastle and arrived at 12:15pm. We had something to eat at a Light-Bites café. The sausages were about ½ inch long, and I got millions of chips over them. It took me ages to find them, and that cost me 27p which I had a good moan about."

I had a couple of secrets that I had kept from my parents, and one was getting my ears pierced on that first week away. Afterwards, my ears really hurt, and the following morning found blood on the pillow at our boarding house. Interestingly I don't remember any comeback.

Further on in my letter, I wrote:

"Fran comes to Newcastle on Wednesday and Thursday, so I said I'll meet her because she's bound to get lost. She just stops on the Wednesday night and goes home Thursday. She's just had her hair cut and set in curls; she looks very mod."

Our mam wrote to Dad regularly, but we don't have any cards or letters written by Dad to her. Maybe these were too personal for her to keep, but he did write to her though. Another letter stated:

"Rosie arrived back early this afternoon from her course, she really enjoyed it and made some new friends. She borrowed my old fur coat to wear as it is so cold and thought she was the cats' whiskers."

Writing to Dad on the 9th of December, Gilly stated:

I'm still on that course and now at the end of two weeks am feeling very tired. Three weeks is far too long to be on that sort of concentrated course. Mind you, I'm not the only one flagging. When you look around, you can see the strain in their faces. I will not be sorry when we go back to the office."

The intensive part of the Civil Service training mainly took part for the whole of December, then petered out into January 1976. We all made friends within the office setting, with some becoming almost like family. All sorts of subjects were discussed, including being constipated. I was shy about using the toilet at work and would sometimes be doubled up in pain. The older ladies would ply me with hot orange juice in a bid to loosen my bowels. Going on holiday was just as bad, often resulting in me not going for a number two for a whole two weeks. At the end of the holiday, I would dash into 19 Hereford Close and sink my grateful bottom onto the toilet seat.

The highlight of our working day was the arrival of the tea trolley. It was a great physical prompt for people to stop their work, take time out deciding whether to buy a chocolate bar, biscuits or scones. Usually, I would buy all three and a cup of tea. This made for a happier workplace, giving us time to chat and take a proper old-fashioned break from work. Unfortunately, it was often crowded around the trolley. As I bent down to get some sweets, a lad called Tom accidentally spilt his boiling hot black coffee all down my back. I was rushed up to the first aid room and was well taken care of. Mam and Dad had taken their first holiday together and returned home to find me wrapped in bandages from the accident. Like I said, work was like family sharing the dramas and shenanigans of everyday life.

Our workplaces were all based around Middlesbrough town centre. The three of us would usually meet up at Victoria Park, unofficially known as the Tittybottle Park, due to young mothers feeding their babies there, happy together sharing lunch in the sunshine. Gilly remembers bringing Mark as a baby and breastfeeding him during our lunchtime break. It was a warm sunny day, and she was wearing a modern white stripey skirt, which ended up covered in poo after his feed. She had to walk all the way back to Acklam, thankfully with the pram in front of her. We would also meet up to go shopping for new outfits to wear at the weekend. We have always been at our happiest when spending time together. We still are.

Whilst working in the Civil Service, you had to have the qualities of a good team player and consequently, office friendships began to grow. I made really good friends within the workplace, one of them being Jo DiGiorgio.

Jo DiGiorgio at Francesca's
Christening wearing my knitted shawl.

She was always doing her fair share of the workload, constantly reliable day in and day out and always answered my never-ending stream of questions with good grace. Jo was expecting her first child, Francesca, who arrived six weeks earlier than planned. So, imagine my surprise to see my sister Gilly, and friend Jo, on the maternity ward at the same time, both with babies in their arms.

A double blessing. I missed Jo's company when she left on maternity leave. Then she decided to leave altogether to be a stay-at-home mum, which was really unusual in those days. After settling well into working life, I remember being shocked at the flirting and life's experiences playing out in the office setting. I worked on the 4th floor and at the other end of the office, one of the married women had given birth to a Down's Syndrome baby – this baby was put up for adoption, and I felt so sad for her. Another close friend came into work crying one day because she had to go for treatment, as her cervix smear had come back positive. One guy found out he had cancer and had to have a testicle removed.

So, being part of a big team, we covered each other's time on sick leave. This would be done in several ways:

1)   Answering the phone and dealing with their case immediately
2)   Sharing out their workload between colleagues
3)   Sometimes, this entailed searching high and low for the client's 'lost' post that was sometimes found in the most unusual places.

I loved working, loved the company and enjoyed my wage going into our bank account each month.

One of Mam's air mail letters to Dad stated:

"The girls are very busy at work, and they are enjoying it more now they understand it better. Rosie gave me a beautiful picture. It is really a copper engraving; I think of Alnwick, and it looks really expensive. Wasn't that nice of her?"

84

As we settled down and learned our roles within the Civil Service, Dad prepared to work abroad in Saudi Arabia. It appears from his CV that work with Horne Bailey ceased in January 1975. His employment history then records work with ARAMCO at a Saudi Arabia Camp Maintenance from 1975-1976. Dad was proud and not a humble man and wouldn't accept a lesser job and knew his value and worth. Francy said a strong work ethic got passed down from his generation to ours, with our parents having firm and strong expectations for their children to follow in their footsteps. They were quite forward in their thinking regarding our education, and it was important that we had good careers too.

A disembarkation card shared details of Dad's upcoming time abroad. His occupation is listed as an

electrician. His address in Bahrain was to be Transit, one of the smallest countries in the world. Yet, still known as one of the wealthiest countries with its oil reserves. The date shown was 24.10.1975.

Hotel Maxim – 03.01.1976

A letter dated 7.11.1975 from P.E.S (UK) Ltd lists the times of the three flights needed for his journey to Transit.

I think money was in short supply as an advance on the salary of £75 was to be paid into their York County saving bank. This causes me to surmise he had been unemployed for a while. Regarding his monthly salary, £350 was to be paid into the above account and £60 to the local bank in Saudi Arabia. Totalling £485 and tax-free, this must've been a golden opportunity not to be missed. He also had to apply for a permanent driving licence to drive within Saudi Arabia's kingdom. I wonder how much of a culture shock it was for

Dad in Al Khobar, Saudi Arabia 46 years

Dad to find himself living within the confines of a deeply conservative Islamic culture?

He had received detailed instructions from his employer, P.E.S, listing the rules for visitors surrounding how life was to be lived in Transit. Prohibited are articles bearing the Star of David (the six-pointed star). Such items are contraband under Saudi laws and will be confiscated. I remember clearly, Dad having a cross hidden at the bottom of his holdall. We must have talked about it after the girls had left home as they have no memory of this. But it gave me comfort knowing he carried this symbol of freedom everywhere he travelled.

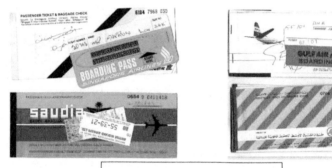

Flight Tickets – Up, up and away!

Alcoholic beverages were also banned, and it was illegal to consume alcohol in public. A letter dated 23.12.1975 has some insight into Dad's life out there:

"Glad to hear all the natives have returned to work, that must have been a wonderful party you were at even though it was only coffee. Hope you can manage a few hours off this week, and don't go cooking meals for all the others. What happened to the rota?"

Another asks:

"How is work going? I bet those Saudis think the world of you by now. I'm sorry you have to work such long hours but the time should pass more quickly. Do you know I still listen for the back door opening about 11 o'clock at night and you walking into the room?"

A few times, Dad brought up the subject of us girls going on holiday in Bahrain. We never took this seriously for various reasons. A trip abroad would have involved us getting inoculated against smallpox and cholera. Gill remembers being frightened and not liking how women were treated in countries like Saudi. She definitely didn't want to wear a burka. This is a long, loose-fitting garment, covering the whole body from head to foot.

The Saudi Arabia government regulations stated women had to dress conservatively and prohibited tight-fitting or revealing clothing. This was strictly enforced in many Muslim countries. Some see it as a symbol of piety, religious devotion, or modesty. This garment appears oppressive to some, serves as protection for others, and symbolises a well preserved middle eastern culture.

Islamophobia really came under the spotlight in the 1970s due to the OPEC oil crisis. The twelve countries that made up the OPEC stopped selling oil to the United States. This sent gas prices through the roof, with OPEC continuing the embargo until March 1974. Throughout this crisis, the Saudis, with British support, softened the OPEC position, providing Britain with relief oil supplies whilst lobbying for OPEC prices to be lowered. Events of 1973/74 helped deepen an already powerful bond between Britain and the Arab monarchs and emirs. Maybe events on TV showed this crisis as a threat to Britain's economy, causing Islamophobia to be thrust into the mainstream, cultivating the fear that my sister spoke about.

Our days were filled with music, fashion and boyfriends, with little thought of politics, the oil crisis or the strikes going on around us. Maybe that was why the decision was made for Dad to seek employment abroad, away from the unrest in the United Kingdom.

The postal workers went on strike in 1971, then the United Kingdom building workers and the miners in 1972. David's employer, ICI, followed with the Grunwick Dispute in London in 1976.

There was the winter of discontent in the UK during 1978-1979, followed by an art strike and ITV dispute in 1979.

There was also a prevalence of deep-seated racist attitudes. These have been well documented, with our country having its own problems right on its doorstep.

But I would like to write a little on the struggles of black women who recognised that their entire community was suffering common racism. These women showed a deep commitment to their cause, joining picket lines causing a black women movement to be birthed. The *Organisation of Women of Asian and African Decent* was a watershed moment in black women's rights activism history. Strongminded women supported each other's differing types of struggles and campaigns benefitting their communities. They confronted problems relating to their children's welfare and black households, highlighting the mental and physical health issues experienced at that time.

During the following decade, the heavy-handed and often brutal police force found themselves tackling the Bristol Riots in 1980 and the Summer Riots of 1981.

Poor economy, high inflation, employment struggle, and the tensions of racism added pain and suffering within these generations. Black parents found their sons being stopped and searched. Police officers misused their powers at a higher rate against black young men than British white males.

These riots shocked Britain, and new schemes were put forward to help young people into work and education, regardless of the colour of their skin.

The only involvement the three of us had with strikes was when the people in the Civil Service protested regarding pay. We had just started our training and would have to cross picket lines to get into work. Gill clearly recalls being called *scab*. A derogatory term used to refer to people who continue to work when trade unionists go on strike wanting a pay rise for their workers. Clearly, we were shielded from the suffering of being unemployed, plus having next to no contact with people of colour, little realised the civil disorder unfolding in the daily lives of others around us. People were becoming hostile towards authority, especially the Prime Minister, Margaret Thatcher, as her policies reduced the power and influence of the trade unions.

A couple of friends remember some personal details during this time. Dawn's account:

"I would return home from school to find candles lit, with sandwiches for tea, until the electricity came on for Mum to cook the evening meal."

Julie's account:

"I was working at The Motor Tax Office and having to work with Tilly lamps that produced bright, warm, white lights as the electricity was turned off. This was most likely the Three-Day-Week. The Prime Minister had introduced measures to reduce electrical consumption, helping in turn to conserve coal stocks, beginning on 31.12.1973. Miners' wages fell, and although a ballot was held to take strike action, it was rejected. An overtime ban was implemented and halved production."

Like the present day, services deemed essential, like hospitals, newspaper shops, chemists and supermarkets, were kept open. Great Britain was becoming the *melting pot*, where different people, cultures and ideas of various kinds would gradually get mixed together.

In 1970, Alexander Solzhenitsyn, speaking at an award of the Nobel Prize for

Literature, stated, "In recent times it has been fashionable to talk of the levelling of nations of the disappearance of different races in the melting pot of this contemporary civilization. I do not agree with this option, but its discussion remains another question. Here it is merely fitting to say that the disappearance of nations would have impoverished us no less than if all man had become alike, with one personality and one face. Nations are the *wealth of mankind, it's collective personalities*, the very least of them wears its own special colours and bears within itself a special facet of divine intention." How true.

Chapter Seven – Wine & Beer Drinking

I n the 1970s, there was a healthier attitude to alcohol, mainly due to drinking being an expensive pastime. Although Dad was often frequenting The Cleveland pub in Linthorpe Village, our parents had strict drinking rules for us teenage girls. We were allowed a Babycham, a genuine champagne perry. Sold in the UK in 1953, this was the first alcoholic drink advertised on British TV. The catchphrase being, "I'd love a Babycham", specifically aimed at women, reached its peak in June 1973 with 144,000 bottles being produced each hour.

Allowed on special occasions and at Christmas time, this tipple was light, frothy and easy to drink. Served in baby bottles, it was posh and sophisticated and instantly recognisable with a baby deer logo.

Our mam never drank, apart from Christmas, and she never drank anything other than port and lemon, as choices were limited. I think she thought that Dad drank enough for both of them and consequently only had an occasional sup with the neighbours. We never set foot in a public house until we were seventeen, nearly eighteen, and even then, Dad took us. My drinking habits started to develop when stepping out into the big-wide-world of work. Added to this was the culture of courting in the pub setting. My husband even got down on one knee and proposed to me in The Red Rose pub.

Turning eighteen years old made it legal for us triplets to go nightclubbing together and to also venture further afield to Beer Kellers in either Newcastle or Sunderland. Drinking lager became the teenager's favourite drink. This was stronger tasting, and Heineken claimed to *refresh the parts other beers cannot reach*. A UK classic to be filmed was policemen being refreshed after a hard day on their beat.

Out and about in nightclubs and pubs

Excessive consumption made for a sore head, but I remember being pleased that I could hold my drink better than David. However, my sister Francy remembers holding me up against a tree for support and then sneaking through the back door of home to put me to bed, so Mam and Dad didn't see how drunk I actually was.

91

I was certainly making up for lost time, and it wasn't until I fell pregnant in 1985 that my love affair with drinking had to come to an end. Thankfully I have never taken up drinking again in quite the same way. Older and wiser as the saying goes.

Back in January 1970, Monday was classed as a hangover day, with people staying away from work after drinking heavily over the weekend. Some older people regard this decade as grey and miserable in many ways, even stating it drove them to drink. Then, like today, teenagers would have disputes with their parents over parties and drinking. A case of *do as I say, good for thee but not for me* was common practice.

Little did I know that alcoholism was a serious concern in the 70s. This resulted from working men's clubs selling cheap beer. Along with the increase in women's consumption of alcohol was their involvement in the nightclub culture. This included us lasses. Shortly before David and I went out together, him and Nicky had been on a drinking spree. This didn't end well as he was jumped by a group of lads and beaten up. He staggered home to bed. His mam got up the following morning to find blood all over his jacket and ended up taking him to hospital as his nose was broken. Just two days later and undeterred, these two lads were found to be knocking on the door of 19 Hereford Close and asking if any of us girls would like to go nightclubbing with them. Of course we would. We piled into David's red VW Beetle and set off to go to the Top Deck in Redcar. It was cold and snowing, but we had a magical time dancing the night away until 2am in the morning.

The Top Deck was a very upmarket nightclub, and we would have to queue round the block to get in. Some young people travelled from Leeds and York to have a taste and experience of this popular club. Once through the doors, customers were greeted by a cloakroom attendant who would hand over a ticket in exchange for their coat or jacket. Just a place to dump a coat, maybe, so you didn't have to walk around with it all night. The noise of the music was deafening as you entered the lower floor of the club. New music from the latest crop of young artists, like Spandau Ballet, Soft Cell and New Order, filled the air. Their music featured a mix of funk, jazz, soul, synth-pop and dance. The best memories were made upstairs, where chart songs,

Top of the Pops editions and party songs were played.

Both floors had special features, décor, and music. L-shaped booths alongside tables and chairs often found small groups of guests making friends with their

neighbours. With ritual practises and rules of etiquette, this sometimes involved sharing drinks and a form of reciprocal drinks buying. An unwritten code of practice allowed a lad to show interest in a girl he fancied by offering to buy her a drink or asking her for a dance.

Such happy memories dancing and partying through the evening with David. I decided I wanted to go out with him, regardless of the fact he was one of the casual interests of my sister. I, too, was already courting a P.E. teacher. This relationship soon fizzled out. David and I began seeing more of each other, and our love blossomed. Besides, having two boyfriends was hard work.

As we shared our lives and pasts with each other, I heard about the start of his working life. He would watch us three triplets walking to the convent, waiting for his double-decker bus to pull away to take him to college.

In 1972, at sixteen years of age, he began a four-year apprenticeship training course with Imperial Chemical Industries at ICI Billingham. He wanted to follow in his dad's footsteps and train to be an electrician, but it was discovered he was colour blind during his medical. So, he began his first year of training as a Mechanical apprentice and won Apprentice of the Year. ICI considered training apprentices very important and provided successful training schemes for no less than fifteen trades.

David's Award, 1st Year Best Apprentice – 1973

This company was founded in 1926 and once upon a time employed more than 30,000 people on Teesside. David said in those days, you could watch hundreds of men and women streaming through the work gates, arriving on bikes, or getting off the double-decker buses. He would get the early morning bus – either the number 41 or 42, that would join this throng of people each day. These employees were involved in making chemicals, plastics, paints, pharmaceuticals, and speciality chemicals. They, in turn, received excellent salaries and pension plans and were expected to keep pace with the latest health and safety techniques. This resulted in their employer having an outstanding safety performance. In the 1950s, ICI developed a fabric called crimplene. This polyester yarn was wrinkle-resistant and kept its shape. This resulted in it being exported to the United States and used by Edith Flagg, a fashion designer. This company was also responsible for advertising icons such as the Dulux paint sheepdog. David was grateful for his training and the education he received, but really enjoyed his life experience from a scheme called ICI Discover. This course was similar to the Outward Bound but modified to suit the requirements of boys and young men employed by this company.

It ran for five weekends, encouraging character building and leadership skills, happily including a trip to the local pub and a weekend in Aviemore, Scotland, in the snow and freezing cold water. Making men out of boys.

ICI Discover Camp – Making men out of boys

After finishing his apprenticeship in 1976, he worked at the Castle Works for ten months before a vacancy came up at Oil Works, where he remained until after the birth of our children in the 1990s.

David was what I was looking for in a man. He was kind, caring and held this secure job, having a great prospect of staying in full-time employment, providing financial security for both myself and our children. In those days, employment with ICI was a job for life, a cradle to grave organisation. Both David's dad and sister were employed over at ICI's Wilton site in Redcar. Alan, David's dad, worked on the Nylon site, becoming a supervisor in engineering works service. Whilst Helen, his sister, was employed as a secretary. She remembers ICI was a good place to work, with a spirit of friendship and community experienced in this very professional company. ICI allowed a lunch break of 30 minutes each day. Whilst in Castleworks, David and some workmates would head to the local pub at lunchtime to down a couple of pints with their sandwiches before heading back to work.

Most drinking still took place in public houses, with men mainly drinking mild ale or light beers. This had an alcohol by volume of only 3%, with stronger examples reaching 6%. Males working in factories or mines would drink pints and pints of the light beers, partially to get rehydrated without getting drunk. Then, because of the long hot summers of 1975 and 1976, lager started selling, becoming the pint of choice before watching the local football match.

It was a different story for women wanting to visit the pub. They would be thought of as brazen hussies going into such a place when they should be in the kitchen getting the dinner ready. Some people thought going into pubs was associated with being common and women were only allowed in the lounge or the big room, not the bar area. Even being in a group was a signal for unwanted male attention. So interestingly, our 18th birthday party was a quiet affair with family and friends, rather than celebrating in the pub. We were given a joint present of an orange and cream coloured record player, along with a Simon and Garfunkel LP called *Bridge Over Troubled Water*. Our two closest friends were sat around the table with us, Julie and Bernadette, with the rest of the evening spent eating, drinking and being merry.

The following year, Dad returned to the UK bearing gifts for all the females in his family. Gold rings and necklaces made of Saudi gold spilt from his travel bag. We had never had such beautiful, decorative items to wear before. We wore our gifts with pride, although ignorant of this country's symbols represented on our jewellery. Symbols of palm trees and crossed swords represent prosperity, which were guarded by these two swords, to defend this nation. Other people would comment on these gifts and recognise their worth, often asking if they could buy them. Until recently, I still had my ring, which I have since passed on to my sister for sentimental reasons. Mam, though, had a very special ring placed on her finger. After losing her wedding ring, Dad had one specially designed for her with love hearts cut into the band of gold. This, too, was made of Saudi gold and treasured by her.

Both Gillian and Ann had met the men of their dreams and wanted a band of gold on their left hands. But to marry back in the 1970s without your parent's consent, you had to be 21 years old. So, at 19 years of age, they asked if they could get married. Good news for one daughter, not for the other. Gillian was given a firm no, and Ann was given their blessing.

21st Birthday Party

In 1975, it was your 21st birthday that was a milestone, your coming-of-age and when you were allowed to vote. One Saturday afternoon found David and me at the Normanby Pub in Eston. This is an area just outside the borough of Middlesbrough. We stopped for a drink and asked if they had a function room to view as it was my sisters' and my 21st birthday in a few weeks. To my delight, we were taken upstairs to be shown a beautifully decorated room. It was expansive and had a central dance floor. I knew it would be perfect for family, friends and colleagues to party the night away, so I booked the date of 18th May 1978.

I arranged to meet up with Francy and Gilly the next week to start planning for our special day.

Soon, the invitations were given out, and we began to worry that this venue would be too small. Arriving early, we decorated the room, and our surprise was Mam turning up with three cakes made in the shape of hearts. Mine had pink icing, Gilly's had green icing, and Francy's cake had grey icing. All had flowers and 21st symbols on the top. Very thoughtful of her.

The food arrived, and we were set to receive people decked out in our party dresses. Mine was cream and had a matching bolero top to cover the fact the fabric was see-through. Both Gilly and Francy had chosen little black numbers to show off their suntans. We were so happy and had beaming smiles all over our faces and had no need to worry as there was ample room for all our guests. I suggested that David bring Nicky along for company to avoid feeling left out, and I could mingle and engage with friends.

The evening was spent dancing around our handbags with people

21st Birthday Party

who we loved. The DJ was fab, playing the music we enjoyed listening to, like *Night Fever* and *Staying Alive* by The Bee Gees, as well as accepting people's requests. I personally don't remember much, as drinks were flowing freely all evening and I got pie-eyed. Amazingly, I now have some photographs of our 21st, after coming across negatives in Dad's old suitcase. I took these to a specialist in Redcar to have them developed. It was like unearthing treasure – such happy memories.

What an expensive year 1978 turned out to be for our parents. Gillian married Neil on 25.2.1978, with Ann marrying Robert on 23.12.1978. Add to that our big birthday bash. Dad must've been grateful to be back in employment with Kearus-Barker Associates Ltd. This spell of work began on 20th February 1978 and terminated on 8th August 1980, the day before my wedding. A letter dated 5.12.1980 states he was there in the capacity of site foreman, supervising his men with authority and fairness, assisting in tasks not generally expected for his position, as well as being an extremely diligent worker. What a lovely insight into my father's character all these years later.

I was now the only daughter left at home, and you would have thought I would have felt bereft, but I was so happy. David had proposed to me. He got down on one knee in the Red Rose pub and asked me to marry him; he didn't know when that would be in the future as we would have to save up. My sapphire and diamond ring fitted perfectly. He had asked my parents, and they were thrilled. Dad's words were, "About time too.".

Life settled down as we both began to save for a deposit for a house, as well as our wedding. Half of my wage paid off my card debts, and the other half went into a joint savings account. A date was set. Nearer the time, I arranged a Saturday to go wedding dress hunting with Mam and Francy. You either went to Binns or a Debenhams store in Middlesbrough in those days. Soon, my dress, veil and shoes were selected, costing a total of £60. The dress was in the sale, half price. We also chose four lilac bridesmaid dresses, and the cost was shared between Mam and David's mam. I remember Marion secretly wanting to make them as she was an accomplished seamstress. The above was the easy part. We had to see the Catholic Priest a couple of times to speak about our commitment to marriage and sign a form stating we would bring up any future children in the Catholic faith. This was because David's family were from a different denomination. Ann and Gillian had previously married at Sacred Heart Church as well. When Gillian was asked by Father Crowley if she was on the pill, her answer was yes. He refused to marry her. Mam bravely went back to tackle the Father about this, knowing there was another couple who he had agreed to marry, even though she was pregnant. It smacked of hypocrisy. Apparently, there was a blazing row, and, somewhere along the line, it was agreed that young Father Keogh would oversee their service.

He was a different kettle of fish and happily agreed to perform Gillian's

Town Square
Billingham
Cleveland County
TS23 2HD

Telephone
Stockton (0642) 553661

with compliments

Billingham Arms Hotel

/00

THISTLE HOTELS

wedding vows. The upset made my sister nervous and worried on her wedding day. However, Father Keogh was pleasant and gently led her and Neil through their service, later joining the wedding party at the reception.

Like most girls, I'd dreamt of a fairy-tale wedding, and our venue was booked at the Billingham Arms hotel. Billingham is on the north side of the River Tees, where we purchased our first home. Our own end terraced house was on Foxton Drive, chosen as it was near David's place of work.

We were both still living with our parents. I remember packing my suitcase a couple of days before the big day and leaving it at our new place. Thoughts ran around my head about it being the right decision. Was I old enough, responsible enough to get married at 23? Would Mam be all right being left with Dad by herself? These worries soon disappeared on the morning of our wedding. David's sisters arrived, looking beautiful in their mauve bridesmaid dresses. I was told that a close relative, Aunty Alice, was too poorly to attend our wedding, but thankfully I had been to visit her to show her a sneak preview of what I looked like in my dress.

I didn't have time to dwell on this news as the car had arrived for the four

MR. DAVID ALLAN GOTT and Miss Rosemary Farrow, both of Middlesbrough, after their wedding at Sacred Heart Church, Middlesbrough.

Sacred Heart Church, Middlesbrough: Mr David Allan Gott, a fitter, son of Mr James and Mrs Marion Gott, of Ravenscroft Avenue, Middlesbrough, and Miss Rosemary Farrow, a civil servant, daughter of Mr and Mrs Frank and Irene Farrow, of Hereford Close, Middlesbrough. The bride was given away by her father and attended by Misses Barbara and Helen Gott, Frances Farrow and Mrs Anne Neave. Best man was Mr Desmond Ladyman.

Sacred Heart Church, Middlesbrough: Mr Michael Cummins

bridesmaids. It was a short journey to the church, and the car soon returned for Dad and me. He was as pleased as punch to have another daughter wed and off his hands and proudly walked me down the aisle. Just before this, found David puffing on his pipe on the back doorstep in Ravenscroft. He was extremely nervous, but as soon as the 10:30am service ended, we both relaxed. The wedding

Married to David – 1980

photos disguised how sad David's family were, but once the pictures were taken, we excitedly set off for the reception. Our three-tier wedding cake sat proudly in the corner of the room, surrounded by the posies and my wedding bouquet.

The one hundred guests sat to enjoy the speeches, buffet and cake. Little did we know that our reception coincided with the Billingham International Festival. Our special day was full of colour, noise and excitement as diverse forms of traditional folk dance, music, and costumes played out in front of our eyes through the hotel windows. This event had been running for sixteen years, and eleven countries were taking part in these events during the week ahead. This was a part of the cultural heritage in that area.

David had planned our honeymoon in the Lake District, and as we had a long journey ahead of us, we made excuses to leave early afternoon. Walking through the hotel doors, we found ourselves surrounded by the parade passing through the town centre and were carried along with dance bands, silver bands, Caribbean steel bands and northern folk. A fabulous start to our journey to Keswick.

As the weather was beautiful, I had packed summer clothes and sandals, looking forward to topping up my tan. Arriving at our hotel in Keswick, we settled in for the night, looking forward to our time together. The weather took a turn for the worst, with summer showers becoming heavier outbursts of rain. After two days of thunder and lightning and rivers of water running down the streets, we decided to set off home. My beautiful wedding sandals were ruined.

It was so exciting to be in our own house, except for the fact we hadn't paid for our TV licence. I was worried we would be caught and fined, but David just laughed, saying, "Who would be out in this weather?" We spent the remaining time of our honeymoon back in Billingham, not letting family know as they would have turned up on our doorstep.

Settling into married life was busy and fun, with the only downside of having to get two buses to visit my family on the other side of the River Tees.

Unusually for me, I hardly spoke to any of the neighbours and was missing my sisters and family such a lot. On weekends, David would be busy doing house alterations. He put in central heating and the boiler and lagged the pipes after the freezing winter of 1980. It was exceptionally cold, getting down to -21 degrees Celsius through the night, causing a pipe to burst in our own loft. I woke to hear water cascading from the ceiling down the stairs. I shouted David, who immediately ran through the freezing water, as naked as the day he was born. The stopcock valve supplying the mains water to our house was under the sink in the kitchen – that was where he was headed. Thankfully, the water never got to the bottom of the stairs, and only the landing and stair carpet needed replacing.

It was Christmas Day. My in-laws had invited us for dinner and didn't bat an eyelid when we turned up early doors after being told about the pipe. Once showered, warm and settled, the men set to discussing central heating boilers and lagging pipes. This event did not spoil our Christmas Day. It only enhanced my love and gratitude towards David's parents. I remember not wanting to go home.

The cold conditions continued, with exceptional amounts of snowfall in late April 1981. Our end terraced house had a gas fire but no double glazing, so there were long brown curtains at every window to keep the house warmer. David also invested in a Calor gas heater and, with it being portable, could be moved to any room in the house. For a few weeks, I kept saying, "I can smell gas", which my husband thought came from the new heater. What we didn't know was he had put some extra tracks in the carpet, which had gone through the gas pipe in the lounge, where the heater sometimes stood. In the end, we called the gas company, who came straight out to fix the problem.

Initially, we bought a property in Billingham as the house prices were much cheaper than on the other side of the river. We both got good wages with ICI and the Tax Office, managing the payments on our £13,000 mortgage well. Still missing family and friends, a decision was made to venture over to Middlesbrough in search of a new, larger property. The next few months were spent searching areas in the outer suburbs of the Boro – Nunthorpe, Stokesley and Great Ayton. Nunthorpe's development began with large houses in spacious gardens with  new housing estates, schools and places of worship built in the 1950s, 1960s and 1970s. This was our area of choice.

Taking David's parents along each time we had a viewing was not a good idea. They dismissed many properties we liked for various reasons. So, one Saturday, discouraged by previous searches, we set off one last time to see if any new properties had come up on the market. Driving through Nunthorpe, we turned onto Ripon Road, noticing a new for sale sign. It stated *view by appointment* only. Not put off, I knocked on the door and cheekily asked if we could have a look around. The owners were happy to accommodate us and allowed us to wander around by ourselves as it was their teatime. I had a feeling of excitement and knew as soon as I stepped in the hall, it was to be our new forever home. We discovered their buyers had just pulled out of the sale, and this couple wanted £25,000. This was too much and more than we could afford, so I suggested we go home, and number crunch our finances. Once back, we arrived at the same conclusion, so I rang Kerry back, offering £23,000 as our best offer. Imagine our delight when it was accepted. After taking Marion and Alan to check it out, we put our house on the market. An older couple bought it and wanted to be in straight away. Managing to obtain a mortgage with the Scarborough Building Society for £19,000, we were left with a six-week window where we had nowhere to live. Our furniture went into storage, and we moved into David's parents' house on Ravenscroft Avenue in Middlesbrough. I absolutely loved living with them. I felt like the Queen as I had never been so well looked after and cared for in my life. Coming in from work, a cooked tea would be on the table, our washing and ironing were taken care of. What was there not to love? David, however, was struggling living back home again, so it was back to our old routine of spending the evening in the Red Rose pub.

I was learning that I had married into a family who showed love in their actions. Marion was capable, intelligent and a virtuous woman, as well as an excellent cook, seamstress and knitter. Her Christmas gift to us all was a knitted Aran jumper, which I loved receiving. Alan was a good provider. Owning an allotment, they always had vegetables and fruit ready to hand. He was also experienced in DIY, often helping David with electrics as my husband was colour blind. For me personally, the time flew by, and it was soon our moving date.

Our new home in Nunthorpe had been built in 1957, with the original sale price of £2,300, unthinkable for a property nowadays. A parade of shops was just around the corner on Guisborough Road, with a newsagent and post office nearby.

To add to this area's beauty was the Cleveland Hills' backdrop, with Roseberry Topping clearly visible through the cut used to access the shops. No wonder I had to practically use a shoehorn in encouraging Kerry and her husband out of 3, Ripon Road. Clearly, she was sad moving, but they had found a bungalow in Great Ayton requiring renovation. This was also a beautiful area to live in.

After they had gone, we looked around and discovered the only items they had left were the lightbulbs. Our furniture and belongings arrived, and with *all hands-on deck*, our family soon had us settled in. We went to bed shattered but happy. We were woken by the noise of the birds. Unbeknown to us, we had inherited two house martin's nests, hidden under the eaves. These are very sociable birds, and we could hear them chattering to each other. Opening our curtains, it was a joy to see them flying around, bringing back food for their chicks. We began to investigate our feathered visitors, discovering these migrants return each spring around the beginning of April from their winter quarters in Africa. They have a wingspan of 29cm and have a maximum weight of 23 grams. Experienced birds remember the location of their territories by sight, with the males arriving two weeks ahead of the females. After laying 4-5 eggs in the nest, the female incubates them, taking up to three weeks to hatch. The parents then spend time dashing to and fro, catching small flying insects, as well as spiders, to feed these tiny, featherless chicks. After five weeks in the nest, these juvenile birds are ready for flying lessons. To our delight, they swooped in and out of the eves and houses, getting plenty of practise at catching insects on the wing. Depending on the weather, after successfully rearing one brood, a second and sometimes a third brood follow. These beautiful, enchanting birds begin to leave in September, but not before leaving us open-mouthed, in awe and wonder about the marvels of migration as they flock together, ready for their journey back to Africa.

There is something wonderful about these natural yearly events of the house martins arriving at our home. Then for nearly six months adding drama, marvel and spectacle to our family's everyday life. After thirty-nine years, we now have six nests instead of two. Our family of feathered friends has grown, with a count of twenty-six chicks, raised and fledged. These birds continue to bring hope and reassurance, giving our hearts a lift in a sometimes fearful and uncertain future.

Chapter Eight – Worth

Shortly after starting full-time work, our only life focus was earning a wage, spending it on expensive clothing and partying the weekend away. Our upbringing had not taught us the value of money, as we didn't have any. This is how it was in the 1970s, and I had some hard lessons to learn along the way. Left with only £2.50 for buying clothes, entertainment and living life, I took out store cards with Debenhams, Binns and Marks and Spencer's. As a result, I was one of the best-dressed girls in Middlesbrough. Quite clearly from Mam's airmail letter, this appears to be true:

"Every week they seem to come home with new clothes or shoes. I'm sure we could open our own boutique. Some of the shoes are ridiculous. If I tried them on, I think I would fall on my nose. But what can you say? It's their own money."

One of Mam's favourite clothes shops was C&A. It was an international chain of fashion retail clothing, operating since 1922. Those stores were a major presence in town centres throughout the UK, employing 4800 staff, of which our Aunty June was one. Labels included: Yessica, Palomino and Clockhouse. Francy remembers we were slim enough to buy from the children's section. A new carrier bag was produced by this store in 1972. The C&A logo was hidden in different coloured dots, which my boyfriend David could not make out. As a new employee in ICI, he underwent a medical check. A report is held that he was diagnosed as having partial colour blindness:

"The above was found to be fit and to have normal vision. He has a mild defect in colour vision. This is not of a classical type, being much less marked, but he does have difficulty when certain colours are superimposed." Medical Officer – 4.7.72

With this discovery, he could not train to be either an electrician or in instruments but ended up doing a mechanical apprenticeship instead.

Another part of the store sold salopettes at low prices, usually bought by parents for their lucky children allowed on school skiing trips. Sadly, the entire British operation of C&A shut down, and the last store closed in 2001. There was a lovely boutique called Sergeant Pepper, selling pretty, floaty dresses popular with young women. I bought a cream patterned dress with a bolero jacket for my 21st party at this shop. My sisters borrowed all my clothes that usually didn't make it to the wardrobe and ended up being dropped on the floor.

Mam wrote:

"Francy has been home this week. She has the dreaded flu. As she was feeling better yesterday, we had a blitz on their bedroom, threw everything out of the cupboard (mountains of magazines and school books) and wardrobe, hoovered the floor and put everything away. They can actually see the carpet now! I might do the same to Ann's room next week."

What I owed on the store cards eventually built up over the next few years. But I didn't see this as a problem until David proposed to me. Francy said this sent me in a complete spin. His upbringing was completely different to ours, and he had been brought up to save his money. I was expected to match his savings pound for pound. Francy and I got our heads together and thought really hard about how to go about settling my debts and saving at the same time. It appeared to be an impossible task, forcing an end to any additional spending to add to my fashion shop collection at home with my cards in Francy's care. My sister cut up each of the cards once my debt had been cleared off. This was a life lesson, and I have never taken out store cards again, other than interest-free offers.

Nowadays, there is a company called Christians Against Poverty https://capuk.org. This is a Christian organisation founded in 1996 and specialises in debt counselling for people in financial trouble. Their mission is to release thousands of families from grinding poverty, treating you as a human being of infinite value. Unknowingly, we value our successes on money, material possessions, and physical appearance, triggering a need to compare ourselves with other people, i.e., *keeping up with the Joneses*.

An iconic must-have growing up in the 70s was the Jackie magazine. The contents covered high street fashion, make-up trends, romance and pop idols. A special addition back in 1972 contained a pull-out centre page of David Cassidy. My sister, Ann, had a massive crush on him. This weekly publication ran from 11th January 1964 until 3rd July 1993 and was the best-selling magazine in Britain for 10 years. Sometimes stated as *a girl's best friend*, it introduced a *Dear Doctor* column in 1974 to discuss below-the-waist issues like the contraceptive pill. This magazine encouraged us to go shopping for fashionable clothes, accessories and makeup.

The three of us would buy each other special Christmas box sets from Binns or Upton's. Estee Lauder's White Linen perfume was launched in 1978 with top notes of Aldehydes, lemon and peach, which reminded me of clean, crisp laundry. It was one of my favourite perfumes back then and was also bought in

Binns store. Walking through this store as a teenager was quite intimidating. The women behind the counters looked beautiful with their faces immaculately made up and looking perfect in their tailor-made uniform and lovely styled hairdos. I would sometimes lose my confidence and walk straight back outside again, to return later with one of my sisters in tow. As teenagers, we would not only be happy to share our clothing with one another but happy to splash out on expensive gifts at Christmas.

Several airmail letters reflect how we loved to bless our siblings. In January 1976,

Gilly wrote:

"Rosie gave me a beautiful silver bracelet, feminine and delicate."

I wrote to Dad saying:

"I got a green shawl from Francy, perfume off Gill."

I was well aware of how lonely our mam was, with Dad working in Saudi Arabia, and I can remember her crying herself to sleep some nights. Perhaps she was exhausted too as that Christmas, writing to Dad, she states:

"I was shattered by Christmas Eve as I had nearly all the shopping to do by myself, not to mention going round with the girls looking for coats. I am buckling at the knees at the moment. I went to work (just one day this week). My eyes won't keep open any longer. It will be a strange holiday without you. It is very lonely sometimes when everyone is out, and it will be worse when Ann is back at college. I love you and miss you very much. God bless and keep you safe."

One of the joys of Christmas Eve was going to midnight mass at Sacred Heart Church. My boyfriend, at the time, was Dougie. Mam wrote it was really cold that night and the church was packed and afterwards something very unexpected happened:

"Dougie was with us and didn't feel very well. When I came out of the church door, he was leaning against the wall, doubled up with pain. Alan phoned for an ambulance, and Rosie and I went to the General Hospital with him. The place seemed to be full of police and men with their faces smashed in. The doctor diagnosed appendicitis, and we were sent up to Hemlington Hospital, where he was kept in for observation. We arrived home at 3.15am."

Writing to my father on 9.1.76, I explained:

"Doug was in real pain, saying he couldn't feel his fingers and that they weren't there anymore. We decided to split up just after that."

Mam had kindly invited blind Mr Devonport to share Christmas Day with us:

"We have asked Mr Devonport round on Christmas Day to share our chicken as his brother is poorly at the moment. Mr D is over the moon about it. The girls have got him a small bottle of whisky, and I have bought him a small box of chocolates. These will be a surprise for him."

Gift giving had taken on a whole new level with the three of us in full-time employment. Now we were able to afford to bless our Mam in the following way:

"Rosie and Francy gave me a lovely cardigan, Snug gave me a red leather purse, and Gill a Roger Whitaker record. I have boxes and boxes of chocolates; they all seem to be Black Magic."

Francy recalls buying Mam flowers and chocolates every time she got her pay cheque and wrote to Dad in January 1976:

"I have received my tax code and hope for a rebate of £70, if I'm lucky, next week. A lot of which is going straight in the bank. The rest is to be spent. A record for Mam, something for myself and little things that I need, i.e., lipsticks."

Our Christmas festivities went well, and Mr Devonport really enjoyed his dinner. Mam writes:

"The chicken was beautiful, and we all stuffed ourselves. Mr Devonport is a very tidy eater and never stopped talking all the time he was here. We had to take shifts sitting with him and listening. It was an absolute joy to watch him open his gifts and guess what they were. I do wish you could have seen him."

Unusually, Mam speaks of receiving a letter posted on 26th January 1976 from Dad, and it only took four days, arriving on the 30th:

"It was fascinating reading your description of the desert, it sounds just like the old movies I used to enjoy. We are all green with envy reading about your adventures."

There is an insight into Dad's wages with Mam keeping him up to date on their finances:

"B Richardson came round after you'd gone and asked if I was managing all right and said he would arrange an advance to tide us over. On the 31st of January, there was a deposit of £410. I hope this tallys with your payslip. Don't go spending all your money in the markets on us, I want you to buy yourself some nice things."

Clearly, Dad took no notice of Mam's advice and bought his four daughters rings and necklaces home from Saudi as gifts. The rings had the coat of arms on of Saudi Arabia adopted in 1950. According to the Saudi Constitution, it comprises two crossed swords with a palm tree in the open upper space between the blades. Each of the swords represents the two kingdoms that founded modern-day Saudi Arabia, the Kingdom of Hejaz and the Sultanate of Najd.

The date palm tree represents vitality and growth. The crossed scimitars symbolise justice and strength rooted in faith. Francy would wear her ring for work and recalls clients offering to buy this unusual item of jewellery after she had explained where it had been purchased from.

Rosemary, Gillian & Frances circa 1974

As we three embarked on our careers, Ann, our younger sister, left St Marys Convent to study for her A-Levels at the Newlands School F.C.J. This college became the only sixth form of its type in the northern region. It described itself as a Catholic college for the whole community. Originally an all-girls school, the convent suddenly became a mixed comprehensive for young people aged 11-16 years. We were the last 18-year-olds to be taught on these premises due to the changes to the schools' admission policies. Seismic changes would be felt throughout this restructuring to a secondary modern high school. Ann recalls that the new catchment area was pretty rough. It was a culture shock for some of her year group, who had to be these *orrible 11-year-old boys* prefects.

Us lofty upper sixth formers didn't have as much to do with these young lads. Gilly remembers these scallywags spitting off the top flight of stairs to see who they could get with their slobber.

Francy remembers some kinder young lads hanging around with the older girls, in a nice way. Maybe they felt safer in this alien environment. I vaguely remember helping out in an art class and only remember how smelly these young kids were.

It will have been very disorientating for the teachers, experiencing this sudden shift between social environments. Time would have been needed for the adjustment, requiring negotiations and alterations to survive and shape new attitudes towards their young charges from less fortunate backgrounds. Ann took 2 A-levels but was required to choose additional topics to fill in her timetable.

As Mam had done typing and shorthand in her younger days, Ann decided to do the same. She really enjoyed the topics, as shown in the airmail letters dated 18.1.76 and 6.2.76.

Mam wrote:

"Snug is getting on great with her typing. Next week she is taking in a form to enter the typing exam in May at Kirby College. Just bought her a new ribbon for her portable."

Ann wrote:

"I've just been to typing at Kirby College, two hours finger work, still I enjoy it very much. Tonight, I did two 30 minutes, getting better all the time! We have started doing letters, envelopes and display work now. It is great fun. Think, now you've got your own private secretary within the walls of your home. Not bad! Always loving you, Snug x."

My younger sister enjoyed the college 6th form, which was much more relaxed than her time at the convent and, as a young adult, was treated like a grown-up. The clothing was freestyle, and she remembers feeling miffed about not wearing the 6th form uniform and felt cheated out of that experience because she had been looking forward to that change. After passing both her A levels (one being Biology), she decided to improve her job prospects. Enrolling at Teesside Polytechnic, she completed a year's course for a Private Secretary's Diploma. A major change had occurred through sixth form and the Polytechnic, in the fact that she wasn't just *the triplet's sister* anymore. Ann was liberated from people's perceived ideas and growing in strength as a capable young lady preparing to embark on married life. The skills taught during the diploma covering accounts, law and business studies were very useful when she began to support her husband as his own *personal secretary*. Definitely not planned, but such a blessing in their lives.

Another skill that young women enthusiastically embraced was the art of learning how to drive. According to statistics, around fifteen million licensed vehicles were on the roads in the UK in the 1970s. Cars had become cheaper and with people's wages increasing, the trend to travel by bus and rail decreased.

In my parent's generation, the distance travelled in Great Britain by coach or bus was nearly 60%, whereas in 2017 passenger journeys on the local bus service is 62% lower than in 1950.

It had previously been a male-dominated pastime with fathers, uncles and sons using the family's car for work or pleasure. Most young men only took three

A gift to dad in Saudi from the three of us

to ten driving lessons before sitting and passing their first driving test. Maybe it was down to the fact that their dad had a car, and they were given access to free lessons. After asking around family and friends, there is a trend of women beginning to take driving lessons as teenagers. But for whatever reason, this new venture was put on hold, often only being resumed when pregnant or after the arrival of children. My neighbour was six months pregnant when she passed her driving test the first time. Often taking several attempts with different instructors, women were told they were *not ready*, which was not good for their confidence. Ann did not take driving lessons until after moving up to Newcastle to live, only after thinking that it would be useful for her to drive before starting a family.

I was fortunate enough to be ferried about on my journeys by David or my Dad. But after having the children and wanting to drive to church on a Sunday, I decided to overcome my fear of driving and began lessons. A lot of money was spent due to needing to change instructors. I won't go into detail as this was for personal reasons, but boy was I happy to pass on my fourth attempt. I got out of the car and jumped up and down for joy. I relished the freedom that driving brought to my life. I no longer needed to pester my poor husband for lifts and realised that driving is a gift.

Driving Licence – Valid 18.04.1996

Interestingly, neither Francy nor Gilly wanted to learn – why would they when they now had their eldest sister behind a steering wheel?

Some interesting transport statistics reveal that the number of licensed vehicles on the roads of Great Britain totalled:

- 15 cars in 1890
- 800 in 1900
- 4 million in 1950
- 15 million in 1970
- 20 million in 1980

There were more accidents/fatalities back in our day until the legal requirement of wearing seatbelts came into force over 30 years ago on 31.1.1983. Cars also have become safer, having safety features built into them on the production line. In reality, road travel is a lot safer, even with over 40 million road users on British roads today. The number of cars on our front drives have also increased over our three generations. Back in the 1970s, my parents didn't own a car until Dad purchased a Datsun Sunny 120Y – David recalls a two-tone purple. David owned a red VW Beetle, and his father owned a brand-new blue VW Beetle that he had purchased in 1965. Unusually, the Gott family had two cars on their drive.

In 1981, 15% of families owned two or more cars, but by 2016 this percentage had increased to over 33%. The number of vehicles at 34 Ravenscroft Avenue increased as David's sisters, Barbara and Helen, passed their driving tests years later. The difference being both girls were given their parent's older cars, possibly having little extra cash due to them completing college and teacher training. David, however, was in full-time employment and could afford to run a car himself. People still find their worth in owning belongings, including cars.

Older generations did without if they couldn't afford it. However, both David and I could afford to buy large household items as a married couple but would save to buy these items outright rather than get things on tick. This younger generation wants everything NEW, NOW, and some are living beyond their means. Some have payments to make on £40,000 cars, alongside mortgage payments of £1000 a month. Sadly, spending or owing more money than one is earning or can repay is a recipe for disaster. I know from my own experience of card debts. But added to this are loans and everything else our digital world has to offer. Maybe you worry about how other people perceive your spending. You have no emergency funds, cannot pay off credit cards or overdue bills. And paying overdraft fees adds to your stress, sadly leading to sleepless nights. There is a quote from Heber J Grant, stating:

"If there is any one thing that will bring peace and contentment into the human heart and into the family, it is to live within your means."

You can help yourself by learning to budget, cut down monthly expenses, start saving funds, be brave, find out how much you owe and create a debt plan. You may need to make lifestyle changes and seek professional help.

A poem written by Minnie Louise Haskins may strengthen your heart to face an unknown future:

Perhaps you are a person who has no idea or doesn't want to know how to put their hand into His? Maybe no one has told you before that you are precious to God, that he made you for a reason and that you are dearly loved. God is love.

I said to the man who stood at the Gate of the Year
"Give me a light that I may tread safely into the
unknown"
And he replied, "Go out into the darkness, and put
your hand into the hand of God."
That shall be to you better than light,
And safer than a known way.

By Minnie Louise Haskins

A poem by Russell Keifer clearly reveals an insight into this love:

You are who you are for a reason,
You're part of an intricate plan.
You're a precious and perfect unique design
Called God's special woman or man.

You look like you do for a reason.
Our God made no mistake.
He knit you together within the womb.
You're just what he wanted to make.

The parents you had were the ones he chose,
And no matter how you may feel,
They were custom designed with God's plan in mind,
And they bear the Master's seal.

No, that trauma you faced was not easy,
And God wept that it hurt you so.
But it was allowed to shape your heart
So that into his likeness you'd grow.

You are who you are for a reason,
You've been formed by the Master's rod
You are who you are, beloved,
Because there is a God!

By Russell Keifer

I had grown up believing in the misconception that my worth and security were found in material wealth. Added to this was an underlying, unspoken lie that the three of us were unwanted, appearing to be a truth after being put in the care of the authorities.

Yet, over the years, I have always had an inkling that we were knitted together in Mam's womb for a reason. Personally, I had yet to recognise that I was uniquely designed with talents, gifts, skills and abilities that even differed from my two closest siblings. Today, I recognise one of these factors is the gift of writing. Deep within me has been a desire to help express in words the deep emotions and hurts that children can travel through in the care system. Yet understanding that other people's life experiences have been far more traumatic than mine, most of which were beyond their control.

Let me encourage you with the truth. You were born for a reason, that the hard times, the ones you want to hide and forget, need to be uncovered. In expressing my past hurts, I hope my honesty will help you speak out about your fears and failures to someone you trust. Don't waste your pain; use it to help others.

Perhaps you could make a list of your talents and abilities or just start serving in your local community. Ask yourself how your life experience shaped you. What special gifts have you been given to enable you to leave a legacy and imprint on the future?

Psalm 71:18 quotes:

"Even when I am old and grey, do not forsake me, my God, till I declare your power to the next generation, your mighty acts to all who are to come."

Each of us is given a unique responsibility to equip and provide for the next generation. My sister Francy has worked for thirty-two years and volunteered in between jobs. She has led by example to her own children and others around her by her strong work values. Even now, in retirement, she is a pioneer, supporting a team who mentor men and women with real-life issues. This group of people are working on an allotment called *Promised Land*, restoring people's lives in a natural, open-air setting, meeting people at their place of need. Work is done in an Eco-friendly way, recycling discarded materials, i.e., wood, metal, plants, furniture and even animals.

She is learning new skills to provide produce for her community, and money is being raised by the fundraising of the sale of fruit and vegetables. This lovely group of people share the land and blessings with local families, even providing land or poly tunnels for others to grow their own food. Another gift she has is sharing her faith, as a Christian, with others around her.

Francy loves litter picking, which often opens doors for people to share what is happening in their lives, good and bad. Blessed with a *listening ear*, Francy often shares people's burdens, providing positive, practical help and advice in her day-to-day life, especially mine.

My youngest triplet sister, Gilly, also has a heart for supporting individuals, family and the underdogs around her, especially those people or groups with less money and power than the rest of society. Time and hard graft are used to deploy her weapons of choice to achieve victory, usually from her bed. My sister has suffered long and hard from a debilitating condition called Myalgic Encephalomyelitis (ME). She has severe cognitive difficulties and often depends on a wheelchair for mobility. There is a very informative website called Action for ME. A phone number is given of 01179279551 to speak to someone from their crisis advocacy and support service if you require help. Living with chronic ill health for over twenty-five years, she benefits from long periods of resting, needed to recharge her body and mind to live her life in the slow lane.

She longs to overcome injustice due to privilege and power, especially wielded by her local council. Over the last few years, she has found herself working alongside her community in the bid to save a green space called Mandale Field in Acklam in Middlesbrough. This piece of meadowland has been used by the local people for years but is now open to unwanted development, due to be completed in the summer of 2022.

It has been well documented that people living in greener, urban areas are less stressed. They have higher degrees of life satisfaction and lower levels of mental distress. Sadly, children's physical contact and intimacy with nature is fading, which may lead to them growing up and not caring for the world around them. It has been documented, by the BBC News in June 2011, that living close to green space increases health benefits up to £300 per person per year. It may yet be proven that our outdoor play helps keep the doctor away. We need people who will fight and help leave a legacy, a green space for future children. Interestingly, no fewer than 462 people have signed a petition against this unwanted building development, which includes a spine road affecting this land, which may soon be given the go-ahead.

There is understandable frustration with this impending decision. Middlesbrough council says it is forced to carry forward decisions made and set within the 2014 Local Plan, blaming past administrations.

I have been given a gift of a booklet called The Ministry of Helpfulness, and in the pages is a poem entitled Recreation:

> *Change from one kind of labour to*
> *another is refreshing;*
> *Change from work to play is*
> *pleasant and healthful;*
> *Change from action to perfect rest*
> *is agreeable and invigorating.*
> *All these changes, made at proper*
> *times and seasons,*
> *are conducive to health of mind and body*
> *but we must be careful to vary the*
> *monotony of labour wisely.*
> *Dissipation is not recreation.*

This little booklet is a compilation of poetry, prose, and anecdotes published between 1903 and 1933. The writer clearly identifies that change from work to play is *pleasant and healthful* and that perfect rest is *agreeable and invigorating*.

What type of legacy does the council want to leave for its future voters? Their actions and decisions now shape what the green spaces will look like in the future. A government policy paper, entitled the *Clean Air Strategy 2019*, sets out plans for dealing with all sources of air pollution, making our air healthier to breathe, protecting nature and boost the economy. Comprehensive actions are set out on how the UK government will protect the nation's health and environment, helping to reduce emissions from transport, homes, farming, and industry.

Alongside this sits the twenty-five-year Environment Plan setting out goals for improving the environment within a generation and leaving it in a better state than we found it. There is a summary of targets on the www.gov.uk website. One states, *making sure that there are high quality, accessible, natural spaces close to where people live and work, particularly in urban areas, and encouraging more people to spend time in them to benefit their health and wellbeing.* Surely this includes having the common sense NOT to build on existing green spaces that have been loved and enjoyed for generations.

In late November into early December 1972, a new political party was formed in Britain. Originally known as The People, its name was changed to The Green Party in 1985. Proclaiming they were neither left nor right, their manifesto contained policies focused on the environment, education, social welfare, pollution, transport, economy stretching right across politics.

The 1970s was a period of rapid change. This party represented a new approach to British politics causing other parties to raise their game, ensuring that the environment stayed a part of political life.

Present day finds this political group in opposition to the Stonehenge Tunnel Plan. A new dual carriageway and a tunnel are planned within the Stonehenge World Heritage site. It is noted that historical evidence of other road-building schemes shows that they do not solve traffic congestion problems. But instead, shift that congestion from one place to another while encouraging further traffic growth overall. Any increase in road traffic is directly contrary to the overwhelming imperative of reducing the emissions driving climate change. This write-up has been taken from the policy, greenparty.org.uk. A clear parallel of direction and interest to the building plans proposed on Mandale Field, albeit on a smaller scale, appears to suggest an identical scenario.

Road traffic has become more of a threat since the 1970s, and children and parents need a whole set of rules to protect themselves from the growing dangers of life outside their homes.

Our residential streets were once the territory and playground of the children where pavements were marked out to play hopscotch and walls used to play football. Once used for games such as Kerby and Canon, the kerb and roadside are no longer available due to the traffic now on the UK roads. However, the game of Kerby has seen a revival and can be played away from the traffic. Purpose-built playgrounds have also been provided, supposedly offering a safer environment for our youngsters but lack the soul of the street and the proximity to their own front door. Maybe it's time to count the cost and the negative impact that *progress* has had on this generation. Assessing the consequences may help people see how past mistakes made our children vulnerable to diseases like asthma, obesity, and antibiotic resistance, which is a serious and growing problem in modern times.

Thank heaven for the people who call others to account for something that has gone wrong, challenging the status quo, especially regarding social or political issues.

Chapter Nine – Weather

As a youngster, I always inextricably linked weather, music and holidays together so that it is impossible to disentangle these life experiences. Holidaying with our parents was done as cheaply as possible. A neighbour, Pat, remembers us as a family walking across the green, carrying plastic bags with our clothing in. She could hear us chattering excitedly about our holiday up to Edinburgh. No suitcases for us in those days. Dad loaded the blue and orange tent and other necessaries, then we jumped into the back of the transit van he had hired for the 158-mile journey. Camping in the 1970s usually involved a ridge, traditional tent for couples, but we skinny lassies managed to squeeze into one. Other families stayed in big-framed tents. The cost of a camping pitch was usually charged per person, but some sites didn't charge at all.

Summer Holidays – Scotland 1972-1974

This year was 1972. We were fifteen years old and Ann thirteen. Giggling with excitement as Dad set off, we clutched tightly to the latticed wooden benches fixed to the inside of the van. Francy recalls rattling around in the back of the van, as there were no seatbelts. The seat belt rule didn't come into force in the UK until 1983, with only the front seat passengers having to belt up under this new law. Mam and Ann had the same sense of humour and what tickled them most was a Monty Python sketch, Miss Ann Elk. They would do the silly voice and fall about laughing, and us three would just look at them, rolling our eyes. An airmail letter dated January 1976, (New Year), states:

"The girls certainly enjoyed themselves this week. They had their friends round, and Tom brought a pile of records, including a couple of Goon LPs. Gerard was in stitches listening to these. There was also a Monty Python record track about Miss Ann Elk and her theory on brontosauruses. Snug and I were in a state of collapse laughing at this."

The back of the van would have blankets, pillows and even a wheeled table for use on holiday. Ann remembers making sandwiches, thankfully without losing a finger, while Dad drove round little narrow country lanes. We would try to outdo each other, describing the most disgusting sandwich filling we could think of to prove how hungry we were. Well into the trip, I recall bursting out with, "I could eat a scabby horse!" I was so hungry and ready to eat anything. The whole family burst out laughing, but Dad got cross as I had distracted him from taking the right

Summer Holidays – 1972-1974

turning. I won, though.

Eventually, we arrived at the campsite. Dad pitched our tent – no fitted groundsheet, no inflatable mattress – just big pins to fasten our blankets to keep us warm. Mam and Dad had the luxury of sleeping in the back of the van, warm and cosy. During the night, it rained cats and dogs. With memories of our tent floating, us girls put on our coats and wellies and went to shelter in the warmth of the ladies' toilet block. That was where Dad found us the following morning. Just going to the ladies' amenities was an education. German women would strip down for a wash, with us appearing rude, no doubt, staring at their hairy armpits and different shaped bosoms. I remember our Mam was a very private person, and I personally had only ever seen her undressed to a petticoat.

Once up and dressed, Dad would cook us bacon and beans on the stove, setting us up for the adventures of the day ahead. I, too, was a bit shy going to the toilets and because of lack of privacy, I could not go for a number two (poo) during the whole two weeks holiday. Of course, four young teenage girls would have the local lads paying us interest. Dad's hands were always full chasing off young men. Boys! Like bees around a honeypot. Apparently, my smart mouth caused enough trouble for the local Scottish lasses to chase after us. They were jealous of the attention their perspective boyfriends were

Summer Holidays – 1972-1974

showing us. They pushed and shoved us down some steps, causing Gilly to graze her knees. Dad came to the rescue and chased them off. The holiday was spent zigzagging across Scotland to follow the sun, as it rained a lot. We have a collection of holiday snippets that have merged, like washing our hair in freezing cold water in the stream, waking up in what we thought were clouds, but was really just Scottish mist.

Several more summer holidays were spent in bonny Scotland where we visited places like Ayr, Perth and Stirling. In Stirling, we visited Blair Drummond Safari

Summer Holidays – 1972-1974

Park, which had only opened to the public in May 1970. I vividly remember Scotland's only giraffes walking near us as they roamed free. We had our picture taken with the camels, Humpledink and Cleopatra, and had a fantastic day at the park. Over 350 animals called this place home – what an education.

On this holiday, we were allowed on a fast army craft, skimming across the water. We were bounced about, making for a very scary ride. One of the lads took a shine to Gilly. Resulting in him motorbiking from Scotland all the way to our house. He had bought her a gift of a watch, and she remembers asking Mam if she could keep it. Her answer was, "Of course you can.". Quite the mercenary attitude.

When we holidayed at Ayr Racecourse, we were blessed with a heatwave. There were limited suntan lotions in those days, and I don't think it crossed our parents' minds to buy such a product. So, we got sunburnt, which no one took seriously. I remember my skin looking brown and cracked like a crocodile, and I still have a t-shirt stripe across the top of my arms. Both Francy and I remember sitting quietly by the water on the beautiful seafront of this popular seaside resort – her writing poems and me sketching birds from a book. Clearly, Scotland was a destination that our parents loved. The journeys home were still exciting, with Dad going round and round roundabouts, pretending he was lost and encouraging the old transit van up hills, like a donkey. Puffing away on his cigarettes, he must have filled the van with smoke, but that too was an accepted way of life. Once home, I would race across the green, into our house, heading up the stairs to the bathroom, hogging the toilet for ages.

Apart from holidays up north, other holiday trips were few and far between. I remember travelling down south to Uncle Colin's and Aunty Pat's home past Birmingham. They had a three-storey townhouse with their living room on the second floor. Very strange. Mam and Dad were given a nephew's bedroom to sleep in, and his walls were decorated with nude pin-ups. Our mouths must have dropped open, and Mam was very embarrassed. I loved it there. We were warm and cosy, well-fed and slept well after adventures around Royal Leamington Spa.

Growing up, we no longer wanted to holiday with our parents, preferring to go with our boyfriends. An airmail letter dated 7th June 1976 informed Dad:

Dave and I are booked up for the 10th – 17th July at Scarborough. I've forgotten what they call the guest house, but Mam knows."

Although I was nineteen years old, Mam and Dad were not at all happy but relented after David's parents insisted that we booked separate rooms. This was during the long, hot summer of 1976. A large high pressure dominated the UK from late May until the 27th of August, when the first traces of rain were recorded. On average, there were more than fourteen hours of sunshine every day. Very different to holidays in Scotland. The hot weather triggered a large increase in the aphid population, followed by a plague of ladybirds. I remember, like yesterday, being stood near Scarborough beach and seeing ladybirds on the floor, the railways, everywhere. There were so many of these seven-spotted creatures. It's been recorded that as many as twenty-three billion were swarming across England's south and eastern coasts. There were so many on the pavements that to walk anywhere, you had to stand on them and crush them. Yuck.

The guesthouse David and I stayed at had a set time for breakfast of eight am. David would knock on the door of my room to make sure I was awake. To his horror, the door of his room blew shut, and I had to get dressed and ask the owner for a spare key. Going down for breakfast, the other holidaymakers burst out laughing as word has gotten around of our dilemma. Poor David had been stood on the landing in his underpants, and now I was bright red and embarrassed.

Rules were strict in those days, and my sister, Gilly, had booked a caravan holiday with her fiancé to the Isle of Whithorn in Scotland. For you to make a booking, you HAD to be married. So, in preparation, she went to Woolworths to buy a *gold* wedding ring. Over the course of the week's holiday, her finger turned green. Scotland is renowned for being cold and wet, so they had packed clothes to suit the weather. Like us, they found themselves in a heatwave.

It was an amazing year with us young ones giving little thought to the country suffering a severe drought. The previous summer, autumn and winter of 1975 were very dry, with some of those months having no rainfall. This led to widespread water rationing and public standpipes in some areas. Reservoirs and rivers were at an extremely low level. For central England, this was the hottest summer for more than 350 years.

Later that year, David and I ventured up to Aviemore in Scotland, staying in the Struan House Hotel in Carrbridge. Our accommodation was about seven miles from the Aviemore centre. It was owned by Karl and Eileen Fuchs, the founders of Scotland's first ski school. We were taken each day to the centre. This opened back in the 1960s, creating an Alpine-style resort in the heart of the Highlands. I remember being in the beginner's class and spending more time on my bottom than up straight skiing. Ski clothes in those days were a bit primitive, and I was wearing jeans. Even though it was summer, there was still enough snow to enjoy. David had been to this ski resort with family and friends and was off skiing confidently down the slopes whilst I was getting covered in bruises. The most enjoyable part of this holiday was using the ski lift. One of those unforgettable moments was breaking through the clouds and mist and finding yourself bathed in sunshine. It was like being on a plane and looking across the earth. It was awesome.

We also went to see the Ospreys at a secret location, which at that time were on the endangered list. David would enjoy drinking the whisky drams lined up for him at the bar when returning to the hotel. A very enjoyable holiday, full of young people like ourselves who were between the ages of 18-35. Alpine holidays abroad were for the privileged few, so this resort was the next best thing.

The weather was still hot and sunny on our return journey to Middlesbrough. David's red VW Beetle overheated halfway home, so we had to stop for it to cool down. He went to find a telephone box to ring his dad and explain we might need to be rescued. After a couple of hours, the car started back up. Back on the road, we kept an eye out for Alan, somehow meeting up with him before the rest of the trip home. His first comment was how tanned I looked and was not at all cross that he had a wasted journey. A proper gentleman.

While Gilly and I were on holiday, our family took day trips to Leeds and Scarborough with the Beeline Bus Company. Mam complained the weather was too hot.

The next holiday for us as a couple was a week in Torquay. This is a seaside town in Devon with a distinctly Mediterranean feel. Amazingly, neither David nor I remember much about this beautiful town, maybe because we drank too much scrumpy cider.

The year after our marriage in 1980, we booked our first holiday abroad to Spain. With no experience of travelling to foreign climes, David and I set out for Gatwick airport by bus. Arriving late evening, we decided to sleep overnight in the terminal. This was a mistake. After hardly getting a wink of sleep, we boarded the flight to Gerona. Sat waiting for the flight to take off, I felt sick with fear and apprehension. Gripping tightly to the seat, I was white as a sheet and endured the two-hour flight, covering the 650 miles from London to our destination.

First Holiday Abroad – Barcelona!

What a joy it was to land on Spanish soil. We quickly located our tour operator and set off for the campsite of Park Playa Bara in Costa Dorada. This area is a coastal region of Catalonia in north-eastern Spain. Arriving at the campsite, we were taken to a brand-new caravan. We settled in for the evening and went to the site's bar for tea. It was my introduction to the Lumumba. This type of cocktail was made with traditional Spanish brandy, and chocolate milk added to it and was an ideal after-dinner drink. I didn't realise how drunk I was until I fell off the stool. We clearly had plenty of lessons to learn about holidaying abroad, and this was to be a baptism of fire. This beautiful campsite was founded in 1970 by Mr Joseph Martorell. It was located next to the Castle of the Kings of Aragon.

Early in the holiday, our peace was shattered after hearing a commotion in the evening air. Armed police were chasing a robber and firing shots in the night

sky, much to our horror. It was very unsettling as this had never happened living in the United Kingdom. The tour operator sold us several trips to tourist destinations, including Montserrat, a Spanish village, Barcelona and Salou. After paying using our travellers' cheques, David decided the prices were a rip-off and vowed to bring his driver's license to hire a car for future adventures abroad. We quickly made friends with other happy campers, eating and drinking and making merry.

The only downside to this whole experience was the hot, smelly toilet. I would quickly shower and dash back to our caravan. Spain was a lovely introduction to travelling abroad. It had an ideal climate, dry and warm, with plenty of sunshine throughout the year. Added to the experience were the fine sandy beaches, typical of the Costa Dorada. What was there not to enjoy? Our trip to Barcelona took three hot hours by minibus, but a walk around the town and harbourfront was a fun experience, and we soon cooled down in our skimpy clothes. Arriving back at the minibus, we were soon whisked off to see a typical Spanish village, an enjoyable end to the day.

By far the most amazing thing we did all holiday was the day trip to Montserrat

Monastery. Incorporated in this experience were the cava and wine tasting. Again, our lack of experience had us tasting raw garlic on toasted bread, and our breath smelled for days. We would not forget Villafranca in a hurry. The cable car from the Montserrat Monastery to the hill area of High Era was spectacular with interesting monuments, like the elephant face and trunk, rising up to the side of us. The Castellet monument and views were breathtaking. Clearly remembered in detail, this fab holiday birthed in us both a love of travelling abroad, especially to Greece.

Come rain or shine, we would be found with books in our hands – something our parents encouraged – alongside our English education. I recall Mam reading

a dictionary as a child for fun. She was an only child, so maybe books were her best friends. Then in later life, Mam and Mrs Greenheld would swap their Mills & Boon love stories to help them escape the humdrum of daily life. Reading also gave us a much-needed break from our busy, chaotic lives, improving our thinking and social skills. Mam and Dad were also avid crossword fans, expecting any of their daughters to give the correct answer to a question when it was fired out at us. You could sense their disappointment if we didn't literally have a clue. Francy said this happened all the time, leaving us feeling awkward and embarrassed.

Our choice of reading material in the 1970s ranged from science fiction, horror, love stories and novels. Most books were borrowed from the library, bought after receiving gift cards from Smiths or swapped between friends. These varied subjects certainly challenged our traditions and customs, helping us to stay mentally fit. As young adults, we all had vivid imaginations, and I remember David taking me to see The Deer Hunter that was released in 1978 when I was twenty-one years old. This was a story of a trio of steelworkers whose lives were changed forever after fighting in the Vietnam War. The script included scenes depicting Russian roulette with a gun – part of a death cult. I was traumatised for weeks after viewing such horror and cruelty. Even today, I can't bear to watch violent films on the television. This film was novelised and published in 1979 after winning 5 Academy Awards, including Best Picture and Best Director. Some people enjoy being scared, and one author that provided horror by the bucket loads was Stephen King. He was a master of creating fear that sticks with us. The writer of Carrie (1974), Salem's Lot (1975), The Shining (1977) and many more novels had me an addicted fan always waiting for his next publication to be released. His readers could relate to the struggles of the characters and the terrors inflicted on them. My friend Dawn told me the horrors would stay with her for days after reading such novels, causing her to hide under the blanket with only her nose peeping out.

As triplets, we would snuggle up in bed to read together the latest novel at that time. Quietly content to be in each other's company until we were called down for dinner by Mam. I vividly recall getting a book called Dune by Frank Herbert, cited as the best-selling science fiction novel in history. I can still envisage the desert planet with nearly no precipitation, with water conserved by *still-suits*. Recycled moisture from the Freeman's lungs, sweat and bodily fluids used for rehydration. But by far my favourite British author was a lady called Catherine Cookson – she is a top-selling novelist. I began reading the Mallen Trilogy, written in 1973 and 1974. I would lose myself in the everyday life and dramas of her characters, as she wrote from the depths of her soul after taking up writing to tackle her depression. This stemmed from her inability to have a child. A stillbirth and four miscarriages pushed her into fifteen years of despair, near suicide and mental breakdown. She was the most borrowed author from public libraries in the United Kingdom for seventeen years. Her novels have sold more than 123 million copies and have been translated into over twenty different languages. After the death of Catherine and her husband, Tom, twenty million pounds from the sale of her novels were gifted to charities close to her heart. The Catherine Cookson Trust was set up in 1977. Her foundation continues to make donations to worthy causes in the United Kingdom. What a beautiful legacy to leave grants to the young and disadvantaged in education, training, arts, culture, environment and conservation.

Sadly, one book remained unread as the priests did not encourage their parishioners to read the Bible. The reason cited that congregations would come up with conflicting interpretations of their own reasoning. Mass was in Latin, but the Bible readings in English had a homily explaining the scripture readings. If you were a regular churchgoer, the church had a three-year cycle of scripture reading, thus hearing the whole Bible over that period. Most families owned

Bibles but favoured listening to it during the Mass.

Mam would have attended religious classes lasting forty minutes every morning during her education, teaching her the basics of the Catholic faith. This rhythm of life spilt into our generation, too, leaving no interest in reading God's word other than in education or during church services. After marrying at the age of twenty-three, I lost interest in my Catholic faith. I began my search for the *Creator of heaven and earth* after the traumatic birth of my daughter, Jennifer, in 1990.

I didn't realise that The Bible is the most read and the most valuable book on earth. The Bible has sold a whopping 3.9 billion copies over the last 50 years. However, more recent estimates put that numbers are at more than 5 billion. The whole Bible has been translated into 349 languages, with 2123 different languages having at least one book of The Bible in their written word.

Have you weathered storms during your life or even in the last year of the pandemic? If so, can I encourage you to read God's message to ALL humankind? It reveals His love and commitment to us personally. What His son has done for us, and how we can live and be inspired by Jesus' simple but powerful teachings. One outcome of the pandemic has indeed taught people worldwide to love their neighbour as themselves, causing us to treat one another as we would like to be treated.

"By him, all things were created, in heaven and on earth, visible and invisible."

This also includes the virus Covid-19. How can this all-loving God, written about in The Bible, allow such suffering that has brought the world to a complete standstill? The most honest answer is that we don't have a clue. Thankfully, the gospel states our hope is to be in Christ who conquered sin and death through the cross and his resurrection. This is sealed with the promise that one day:

"He will wipe away every tear from their eyes and eliminate death entirely. No one will mourn or weep any longer. The pain of wounds will no longer exist, for the old order has ceased."

In hindsight, we can see that individuals' joint efforts are beginning to defeat the Covid virus in our generation. Acts of courage and self-sacrifice have been an inspiration to others. What each of us does each day has a ripple effect on the lives of others around us. Kindness, courteous behaviour and sympathy can be infectious as we share life's challenges openly and honestly. I can honestly state that I have needed to draw strength from my Christian faith. Struggling with the issues brought on from the pandemic forced me to seek God in a deeper way, looking to the promises held in His word and praying for hope in these dark times. My prayers have expanded to include other countries and faiths to have healing and strength in the face of diversity.

The past year has taught me to count my blessings, recognising the preciousness of immediate family and the value of ordinary people working in caring roles around the country. It's strange, isn't it, that we don't remember the wet summers as much as the dry, sunny days spent with friends and family?

Everything appears clearly defined in hindsight, like getting the bus to Great Ayton and walking for hours in the countryside, picking brambles along the way. On one such adventure, I remember insisting on wearing my new shoes that had a wedge heel. After miles of walking, blisters formed on my skin, which had me resorting to walking barefoot on grass and paths alike. I'm sure Dad would have reminded us about a story when he was a lad. He would get up early and lick the road wearing nothing on his feet!

One tale he told that wasn't tall had some unbelievable elements to it. The Farrow family lived in a small cottage at Fairy Dell on the outskirts of Middlesbrough. It was 1939. War was looming, and the older children, including Dad, found themselves being evacuated to the coast at Scarborough. Dad and several of his brothers hated being away from their mother and undertook the forty-eight-mile journey back home on foot. Hiding in the countryside, these scruffy little urchins would somehow find their way home. Several times the authorities would try to part this family until it was decided it was safer for them to stay in the care of their mother. Their little cottage did get hit by a bomb – it came straight down the chimney but didn't explode. Woken by his older sisters and in his little nightshirt, he was made to walk past this smouldering bomb to safety outside. No doubt, these youngsters would be found in bombed-out areas near their homes, playing games with toy guns and pretending to be dead. Cops and Robbers, Cowboys and Indians kept them entertained for hours on end.

Energetic boys would be found making go-carts or sledges out of little more than planks of wood, a set of old pram wheels and lengths of rope. Surrounded by dereliction, these items were part of everyday life, and so was taking your life in your hands. Dad would recall being able to sledge in the snow, nearly all the way to Middlesbrough from home. This covered nearly five miles downhill, only then having to trudge all the way back. Clearly, there was a lot less traffic then. This once leafy suburb now has so much traffic travelling on this main arterial route into Middlesbrough that it has been dubbed the Marton Crawl. It is a nightmare for commuters as well as people trying to get access to James Cook hospital. This is a designated major trauma centre equipped with its own helipad, helping the air ambulance service make a real difference in the delivery of care by having access to a specialist trauma team as quickly as possible. No matter the weather or time of day or night, it has been a blessing to have this hospital down the road. On reflection, the staff have provided emergency care and help in my family's time of need. From split lips, broken arms, operations, cancer care, maternity care, needing x-rays, CAT scans, major surgery and blood pressure treatments. This cradle to grave organisation has covered our life's dramas with wisdom, expert skill, knowledge and competence.

I was so grateful for my father's care, especially in his later years, that I decided to volunteer in the hospital's main café. After a year of waiting on tables and cleaning up, I had the opportunity to do Chaplaincy training, thus, enabling me to visit some very sick people on the wards. Walking into a room, I began to speak to a patient and his wife. I was a nice distraction from the stress of waiting for his impending brain surgery, and this couple began to ask about me and my upbringing. He had a connection with Park Road North and knew about Nazareth House. After sharing part of my story of being a triplet and being in the children's home, he looked me straight in the eye and told me, "You begin from the beginning". Both he and his wife were the catalysts that seemed to propel me forward in making the decision to pick up my pen and begin to write my story.

That afternoon after returning home from James Cook, I sat on the settee and prayed to God for help if I was to do this task. The strangest thing happened. I can only describe it as receiving a download from heaven. Immediately, I knew the book would have ten chapters, and all the chapters would have a heading beginning with the letter F. My mind was flooded with memories, and I was compelled to pick up my pen to write. It became clear that I would need to begin researching our past history, which was quite painstaking at times. But in 2016, my first book, *3 Peas in a Pram* was published.

Interestingly, the encouragement to write book two, *3 Peas in the 70s*, came from my daughter-in-law's family in Bangladesh. James had married Rumana, a Muslim girl whom he had met at university. Her family came for a short stay in Middlesbrough, and it was lovely to be a part of their lives, if only for a short time. I posted a copy of my book, hopeful that it would arrive safely at their address in Dhaka. It did. Her father, Mushtaque, wrote back saying:

"I have read and thoroughly enjoyed your book. What an interesting glimpse into your family background. You must have done a lot of research to produce it. Rum tells us about the hard work you've put into publishing and promoting it. That is inspirational!
We would encourage you to write another volume. Which is why we are sending you a little something (a leather document holder) to store your scribbles and notes. Hope it comes to use.

Warm regards,
Mushtaque, Ahmed and family."

I wonder where the encouragement will come from for book three? Only time will tell.

Chapter Ten – Wishes on Reconciliation

In writing this second book, I have had to take a trip down memory lane, mainly recalling pleasant and sentimental memories. However, I found myself returning time and time again to the echoes still heard in my mind of

Nazareth House

our past experiences in Nazareth House, with such a longing for me to be reconciled with my past. To help with this process, I previously put steps in place for my sisters and me to return to the children's home with a family friend, Bernadette. February 2014 found us standing in front of the massive doors. After ringing the doorbell of this listed building, we received a warm, friendly welcome. We were invited to have a look around our childhood home. Interestingly, both memories of the home and chapel merged together with school and church. My confusion began to clear when I looked out of the top window down onto the courtyard below and realised it was very much like the playground of Sacred Heart school. All these places were identical, and as an adult, I realised that my memories had combined as one. The young lady giving us the tour took us up to the top floor dormitory, where we would have slept as young girls. Looking out of the window, I could see Albert Park. There was a separate door in the corner of the room, where we were told the nun caring for the young children would have been. As I entered this small room, the only thing I was aware of was the smell. It made me want to run from the place, so I turned and walked out. After saying thank you to the young lady for our tour, I was interested to hear what my sisters had experienced. Chattering away in the car with Gilly, Bernie did well to keep up with all her questions. My sister was buzzing as she had expected to feel lots of negative emotions but actually found the timing of the visit just right. After dropping Gilly and Bernie home, I questioned Francy, who had been really quiet – not like her at all. She felt sad and upset for all the other children who had been through the home. We had heard rumours of ghosts, babies crying, toilet doors opening and closing, all of which were very unsettling.

Four years later, I found myself talking to a social worker who gave me the following account:

"As a social worker, I had a young woman who needed somewhere to live during the later stages of her pregnancy and the early weeks of her child's life. The only place available was Nazareth House in Middlesbrough. I remember the building as very austere, with linoleum floors in the girls' rooms, metal-framed beds with thin mattresses. Very little feeling of warmth about the building. The sisters were formal in their dealings with the girls and visiting social workers. They gave the

impression that the girls had transgressed. Rules were rigid, times to get up, rotas for chores, mealtimes, evening curfews and bedtimes. I worked hard for reconciliation so the young woman I was working with could move back to her hometown and family."

I was never told the outcome of the above story, but you can clearly imagine from this account that there could be a lasting effect on those who have spent time growing up within the walls of this orphanage.

During my research, I have spoken to many people, who after living here, experienced heartache and trauma to the degree that caused some:

- To never set foot back in church
- Others who have NEVER told their family that they were brought up in this children's home
- To have a fear of nuns
- Never to speak about it, like our mam and dad
- To be haunted by dreams and memories
- Parents to live with the guilt of putting their children in care
- To be fearful and resentful
- To need counselling; with others self-harming as adults, to ease the pain of past memories
- To seek revenge
- To never read the Bible

The overwhelming emotion for me on that return visit was fear – I had a fear of demons or ghosts from the past. But, as I sat quietly and prayed, I sensed God taking me by the hand and then walking me back into that smelly room. He lifted me up in his arms, where I felt safe. The demon had to kneel in God's presence and, as I watched on in amazement, I was no longer fearful.

There is a scripture in the Bible that says:

"The authority of the name of Jesus causes every knee to bow in reverence."

***Philippians 2:10**. God longs for you to be reconciled with Him and with your past, so you can walk into the future He has planned for you. You are precious to Him regardless of your own personal life and history. For some, reconciliation is a new concept but simply put, Jesus bridged the chasm between God and us. He lived, died and came back from death, so we can come to God directly, helping in the restoration and re-establishment of friendship and harmony with him and those around us.*

Can I encourage you to call on the name of Jesus and read the Bible? These actions will help *set in motion* the wrecking ball needed to bring down those high towers of fear and pain built up around you. His promise is that He will bring healing and make all things new. Healing takes time, so be kind to yourself and seek help if you are overwhelmed.

I have put together a list of organisations/help groups in the index at the back of this book.

One of my closest friends, Bernie, lived just along the road from Nazareth House. She would come and visit us in Hereford Close. On warm sunny days, we could be found sunbathing on the brick, wash house roof. It was quiet there, and no nosy neighbours could watch us. A few of these times, Julie Brodick would join us. Aged around fourteen to fifteen, we all had steady boyfriends, often spending many happy hours in each other's homes as couples. Julie recalls going nightclubbing too. As relationships blossomed, one of our older friends fell pregnant at seventeen. I remember visiting her after the birth of the baby with little understanding other than the baby was on the inside, and now the baby had *come out*. My friend, thankfully, didn't enlighten us. After pegging the nappies and baby clothes on the washing line, she complained I hadn't done it properly.

Back in the 1970s, there were rules to be followed on the labour wards. Husbands were only permitted during the first stage of labour. Smoking was strictly forbidden. No food or drink, of any nature, on the ward, and he must be ready to leave promptly if asked. New mothers had to follow the maternity ward rules too. Children were allowed to visit, but only husbands were allowed in the room while the baby was fed. Peace and quiet were needed for satisfactory feeding. Baby would be returned to nursery for supervision at night with set feeding times. These rules – and more – were set in place to ensure the infant received the care and feeding required for development and to ensure a speedy discharge from hospital. After most births, the mother was to spend at least a week in the maternity ward.

After my mam gave birth to us triplets, I was soon discharged after reaching six pounds in weight, whereas Gillian and Francy would have been kept in the premature nursery. They received special care, and the rules were stricter. Only the parents/patients were allowed to visit. The baby, or babies, were not to be handled without permission. If there were any individual requests, permission from the sister in charge would have to be given.

The hospital staff had some difficulty in rearing my two smaller sisters but, by August 1957, all three of us were in excellent health and back together again.

Anthony, our cousin, recalls being a frequent visitor to Hereford Close around fourteen and fifteen. He said the motivation was because we knew lots of girls from school, and it was an interesting, hormonally charged time in his life. He would find himself naturally tagging along with Dad and us on trips to

Billingham's old baths. He received a ticking off by Dad after commenting on a lady wearing a white bikini, which turned see-through after getting wet.

As friends, we would pile on the number 42 bus to Billingham Forum to go ice skating, making us feel very mature and grown up on such an adventure. Anthony said, "You always appeared to be more level-headed than I felt, certainly more sensible." By this time, he attended St Michael's secondary school but saw his education as more of a social activity. His parents were trying to keep their son out of public houses with little success. This no doubt led him to leave school with only a handful of pointless CSEs, receiving little guidance into the world of employment. After unsuccessful jobs in shops, he enrolled in Kirby College and went on to join the Airforce in Weston-Super-Mare. Thankfully, the penny dropped that he would require five O-Levels for any meaningful job. In his early twenties, he sat Maths, English and Physics, providing proper qualifications.

Even though we were related, only Francy recalls us going to Anthony's home on Devonshire Road, and that was because Aunty Celia fed us eggy bread, which the posh people call French Toast. Clearly, we had never eaten this before. Eggs and milk are added to a bowl and whisked up before dipping bread into the mixture and then fried in a pan. Yummy!

After leaving full-time education, we'd kind of lost touch with Anthony, only occasionally seeing him on our doorstep. In an airmail letter dated 10th March 1976, Mam writes to Dad stating:

"We had a very rare visit from Anthony Butler the other evening. We had met him down the town, and I honestly didn't recognise him. He was in uniform with short hair and dark-rimmed glasses and putting on a posh accent. I don't know how I kept my face straight. Apparently, he is stationed near Scarborough, works 14 hours a day for four days, then has four days off. Can you imagine it?"

Fast forward. With the publication of *3 Peas in a Pram*, this eloquent cousin with the posh accent told me, "There is too much of God in this book.".

No doubt that will be Anthony's cry again, sitting down to read this publication. But I want to tell you, God is a God of the second chance. He wants to restore the years the locusts have eaten. I want to write words on these pages to breathe sweet encouragement upon downcast souls. To be an agent of reconciliation and peace in the lives of my readers.

Have you ever considered that your past is holding you captive, making you live your life in fear?

I can recall taking driving lessons in my thirties and feeling fearful most times sat behind the steering wheel. This continued for months, then my instructor told me I was ready to take my test. Feeling sick with apprehension, I failed three of the tests. But something changed on my fourth time of trying. As I was getting ready that morning, words came to mind of:

"There they were, overwhelmed with dread, where there was nothing to dread."

On arriving at the driving centre, I was waiting for my name to be called. A quiet gentleman (who I had never met before) called my name, "Rosemary Gott". Getting into the car, my heart was pounding in my chest. It started to rain, and I was so grateful to have been shown where the windscreen wiper switch was in the previous session. After being asked to reverse between two cars on a wet cobbled road, I found to my horror that my wheel had touched the curb. In my head, I was convinced I had failed, and strangely this caused me to be less stressed. Travelling back on the dual carriageway, the instructor asked me to take a sharp left. After signalling and looking quickly in my mirror, I travelled down the ramp. Arriving back at the centre, I was asked questions on the highway code and answered as best I could. I could see him scribbling on a sheet of paper, which he then proceeded to hand me, saying I had passed my test. I didn't believe him. Asking my driving instructor to check the paper, he confirmed that I had passed fourth time. I was so happy and began to jump for joy, thanking God.

It was not until many months later that I discovered the words that came to mind that morning were written in the Bible, and came from Psalm 53, verse 5. The word *dread* in Hebrew can also mean *fear*. In my own foolishness, I had suffered both. Yet, these words had also brought me comfort. I had been given the grace to face this fear with the power of God's promise.

My prayer for you is to be touched by God's grace. Grace is the love of God shown to the unlovely, the peace of God given to the restless, and the unmerited favour of God. Grace is most needed in the midst of brokenness, sin and suffering.

Jesus says: *"Come unto me, all ye that labour and are heavy laden, and I will give you rest."*
He also says, *"Him that cometh to me, I will not cast out."* How he loves you!

Are you afraid to die? Give your fear to HIM. I have come across a poem titled:

Are You Going Home?

Let me tell you that you do not have to be afraid of God, nor afraid of your past. He longs to be reconciled to you, for he came for the lost sheep. Can you grasp how high, how wide and how deep His love is for His creation? You are His creation. You may think that dealing with the past could open a whole can of worms, causing a complex situation to produce subsequent problems that are unpleasant to deal with or discuss. The truth may well result in your problems having no easy solution. But how can you love your neighbour if you don't love yourself?

"Are you going home to be with the Lord?
You are not afraid, are you?
Afraid of what?
To feel the spirit's glad release,
To pass from pain to perfect peace,
The strife and strain of life to cease?
Afraid of that?

Afraid of what?
Afraid to see the Saviours face?
To hear his welcome and to trace
The glory gleam from wounds of GRACE
Afraid of that?

Afraid of what?
To enter into heaven's rest
And yet, to serve the Master blessed,
From service good to service best?
Afraid of that?"

I know from experience that dealing honestly about the past is painful, but I hope that sharing our past secrets makes it easier for you to tell yours. Isn't that what family should be about? You need to know you are not journeying alone. We are on this journey together. It has been a real commitment to put my life on hold to put pen to paper, but I know that speaking about the past brings healing to past failures and silences traumatic thoughts. Seek help, share your deepest sorrows, shame, burdens alongside your desires and greatest joys. A true professional will help you honour the gifts of the past and tenderly confront any agonies that originate there, helping you learn new ways to heal and grow.

Sharing your own personal history can be an intensely emotional experience, as I know full well. But put your hand in God's and ask him to show you the way forward. I did. Then go into the future with a fresh new objectivity, after being helped to see your situation from a more accurate point of view. Everything looks clearly defined in hindsight when we can understand past events.

Recently, a friend of mine apologised for something that happened in my past, when actually it was nothing to do with her. This had a profound effect on

138

me, and I started to cry. So, I would like to say sorry and apologise for:

- Words of cruelty that were spoken over you
- The wrong attitudes due to the colour of your skin or denomination
- For the times you were made to feel inferior for the clash of different cultures
- The times you were made to feel unhappy and ashamed
- The times you were in chains of oppression, shackled to your past
- The time you were pushed into being involved with cults
- The times you felt used and disregarded
- The time you were left by yourself, through no fault of your own
- The times that people controlled your life, not allowing for your point of view or your past mistakes
- For the times when arrows pierced your heart, causing pain and wounds that festered over time.
- The times church family made decisions that broke your heart, causing you to leave and walk away from your faith
- The times family, people or friends betrayed their trust in the dealings with you

Have you heard of Psalm 23, headed:

'The Good Shepherd'?

"The Lord is my best friend and my shepherd.
I always have more than enough
He offers a resting place for me in his luxurious love.
His tracks take me to an oasis of peace,
the quiet brook of bliss.
That's where he restores and revives my life.
He opens before me pathways to
God's pleasure
and leads me along his footsteps
of righteousness
so that I can bring honour to his name.
Lord, even when your path takes me
through
the valley of deepest darkness,
fear will never conquer me, for you
already have.

*You remain close to me and lead me
through it all the way.
Your authority is my strength and my peace.
The comfort of your love takes away my fear.
I'll never be lonely, for you are near.
You have become my delicious feast
even when my enemies dare to fight.
You anoint me with the fragrance of
your Holy Spirit.
You give me all I can drink of you
until my heart overflows.
So why would I fear the future?
For your goodness and love pursue
me all the days of my life.
Then afterward when my life is
through,
I'll return to your glorious presence
to be with you forever."*

Jesus is your Shepherd. If you feel like a sheep without a shepherd or have lost your way, seek Him. He's been calling your name. In the Bible, He promises:

"Behold, I myself will search for my sheep and seek them out, I will care for my sheep, and I will deliver them, I will bring them out and gather them, I will feed them, and I will lead them to rest, I will seek the lost, bind up the broken and strengthen the sick."

He will come, find you and bring you home.

These scriptures held true for my parent's generation. Dad was raised as a protestant, going to the imposing *Big Wesley* on the corner of Linthorpe Road and Corporation Road as a child. This building stood proud after being built in the 1890s and was sadly demolished in 1955, making way for the British Home Stores shop on that site.

Francy remembers Dad sharing with her that his all-time favourite hymn was The *Old Rugged Cross*. I think the lyrics from this traditional song brought Dad comfort in times of suffering and despair.

The Old Rugged Cross

"On a hill far away stood an old, rugged cross,
The emblem of suffering and shame,
And I love that old cross where the dearest and best
For a world of lost sinners was slain.

So I'll cherish the old, rugged cross
'til my trophies at last I lay down
I will cling to the old, rugged cross
And exchange it some day for a crown

To the old, rugged cross I will ever be true
Its shame and reproach gladly bear
Then he'll call me some day to my home far away
Where his glory forever I'll share"

Like a lot of popular hymns, this is universal and timeless, grounded in scripture with a great melody:

When Dad was on end-of-life care in James Cook hospital in April 2008, he asked me to bring him two wooden crosses. One for him and one for a friend on his ward. Maybe he had this hymn in mind as he waited to go to *his home far away.*

Different generations, involved with different denominations yet sharing broadly similar beliefs, practices in the branches of Christianity, this was our family's religious makeup. Mam's Catholic upbringing spilt over into her daughters, causing us to live in a cocooned environment. So much so that after completing her R.E A-Level at eighteen years of age, Francy considered becoming a nun. She cites this being due to a couple of reasons: her R.E. teacher, Sister Marie, was a shining example of what a nun should be, and she also had an increased awareness of God from studying the Bible. However, later in life, she became conscious that there were other ways to serve God. Personally, there was as much chance of me becoming wed to the Catholic faith as a blizzard in July.

So, in my thirties, I began my own search for God and became a born-again Christian after being invited to the local Baptist Church by a friend. My children were also influenced by their Christian upbringing, making their own decisions whether or not to follow in their mother's footsteps. That choice is also yours to take in the time that you have left on this earth. Time is precious, and our eternal welfare depends upon it. Have you ever considered that the time given is in order for you to prepare for eternity?

Perhaps, on reflection, one of the gifts of the past is to remind us that no one lives forever. I recently came across an article written by the teessidecharity.org.uk. It was dated 31.7.2017. A man named Eddie White had his voluntary efforts recognised with a Teesside Hero Award.

Looking at the photograph of this eighty-four-year-old, I recognised him straight

Youth Club

away. He was the kind gentleman who returned me back to my parents at fourteen years of age. He had listened to why I had run out of our house, quietly insisting that my parents would be concerned about my whereabouts. The write up includes how some people told him that the youth club kept the kids off the streets. But, for Eddie, it was more important to keep the youth on the straight and narrow, help them respect the premises, other people, and themselves, with the club hopefully having a positive impact on them. Clearly, this youth worker has made an impression on me because he recognised that he had a responsibility to put something back in helping the young people around him. The article went on to quote Eddie, saying:

"If something needs doing and we can help, we shouldn't leave it to other people."

This youth club opened back in the 1940s, originally as St Philomena's Boys' Club, changing its name to Sacred Heart Youth Club in the 1960s. Neither Mam nor Aunty Celia would have been involved with this club as it was only in 1965 that girls were first allowed to be a part of it.

Mainly catering for young people around the ages of nine to eleven, we found ourselves at the doors of 364 Linthorpe Road on a Friday evening for the disco. I mainly recall the paint peeling from cream walls and the tuckshop where you could spend your sixpenny bit (6d) on sweet treats. Us kids would play football, pool, table tennis, board games, and dance the evening away with girlfriends.

Sadly, Eddie died in December 2019, but he had left a legacy of volunteering. He spent thirty years as a youth leader, raising money for the Sacred Heart Church, building funds and caring for the lawns, hedges and plants around the church's grounds. He was a well-respected, unsung hero of his day, representing all that is best about Middlesbrough. A man who had clearly spent his time allotted well. Recognising that life and the club's real success had been to consistently turn out good, solid citizens in each generation, loyal to their Christian faith. All in some way are seen to be better for having been members, as we indeed were.

This life experience was beyond the children who were raised in Nazareth

House. However, I recall being told that the young teenage girls would walk to Sacred Heart Church, when not at school, to help with the cleaning and polishing of the inside of the church. They would have no doubt been very experienced in these chores, as the building they lived in was huge. Built of smooth red brick, Nazareth House was an imposing building, two stories high, having a thirteen-bay entrance front. It provided accommodation for hundreds of children and nuns. Clearly, from our entry numbers of 2780, 2781 and 2782, hundreds of children had passed through these doors. The building needed cleaning, and some of these jobs would be expected to fall on the shoulders of the children living within those walls.

I recently spoke to Paul Tasker, whose dad was a caretaker and gardener of Nazareth House. He recalls his father having to take two jobs to feed his own large family of ten. Invited to eat within the walls of Nazareth House, he remembers seeing children on the streets, queuing up outside churches. This was in the 1960s, and when he questioned his dad, he was told the children were waiting to be fed as it was the summer holidays. This appears to confirm that we, as children staying in the children's home, were better fed than *outsiders.*

As I bring this book to a close, I can sense familiar emotions rising up in me, linked to the depression that my Mam suffered throughout most of her life. Quite clearly, as children and young adults, we have suffered from the fallout of such an experience. The natural results of living with a depressed person bring sadness, guilt and resentment. I now understand that many people live with confusion, self-doubt, and demoralization and long to escape from such a relationship. But as my mother died in 2008, she no longer lives or carries that depression with her. I don't have to either, and neither do you.

I remember my father's rendition of *Zip-a-dee-doo-dah* by Steve Brock:

"Zip-a-dee-doo-dah! Zip-a-dee-ay!
My, oh my what a wonderful day
Plenty of sunshine heading my way
Zip-a-dee-doo-dah! Zip-a-dee-ay!
Oh Mr Bluebird on my shoulder
It's the truth, it's actual
And everything is satisfactual
Zip-a-dee-doo-dah! Zip-a-dee-ay!
My, oh, my it's a sunshiny day
There's plenty of good times
Heading my way
Zip-a-dee-doo-dah! Zip-a-dee-ay!
Wonderful feeling
Feeling this way."

Another favourite song of my parents was by Vera Lynn. She was *The Force's Sweetheart*.

As the United Kingdom was in the middle of the conflict of World War Two, Vera was singing to and about the brave air force pilots, expressing optimism and victor for those fighting on the side of *truth*. This song was written by an American, Walter Kent, who did not know that bluebirds didn't fly over the White Cliffs of Dover. However, these birds are seen as a symbol of hope, much like having Mr Bluebird sitting on your shoulder.

The bluebird is also referred to in The Message Bible:

Cranes know when it's time
To move south for winter
And robins, warblers, and bluebirds
Know when it is time to come back again.

Can I encourage you that there are indeed better days ahead? Summer is nearly here, and my husband has seen two house martins flying in our area. Like the bluebirds, they know when to return home and prepare nests to raise their young. I, for one, can't wait to see these beautiful birds again, bringing with them hope, joy and drama into the months and years ahead.

With these words, may I offer a prayer:

"May the Lord bless you
and keep you.
The Lord make his face
shine on you
and be gracious to you
The Lord turn his face
towards you
and give you peace."

Once again, I have written down what my sisters and I remember about our past. This book is a collective autobiography and will hopefully give you an impression of our rich social history, passed on from generation to generation.

Acknowledgements

This has been a year to remember, with the world and the United Kingdom forced to come to a grinding halt due to the pandemic. Lockdown has refocused my mind to complete the task of writing *3 Peas in the 70s*. I have reaped the rewards of tapping into my sisters' memory boxes. I am grateful for the precious support in recording the highs and lows through three generations.

We are grateful that amongst our parents' belongings were found airmail letters written during Dad's employment abroad during the 1970s. Who knew that this old-fashioned way of communication would be integral and essential in writing this book? Encouragement sometimes comes in a very practical way. This support showed itself through my husband, David, cooking and supplying me with endless cups of tea, helping me to remain focused on the task in hand. Thank you. This was also revealed through the people who took the time to fill in my questionnaire, sparking into life my imagination about the olden days. Talking about the past, cheers to Robert for the finer details into Middlesbrough Football Club during the 1970s, who has supported this team through the good times and the bad. It has been a delight to sit and listen to the snapshots of Grandad Leo's life and personality provided by Joyce and Joe Harland. Who knew you would one day be reunited with one of your landlords' granddaughters?

Thank you, Dawn, Celia, Carol and Tracey, for the prayers and encouragement offered up during the period I have been writing this book. You have all been a Godsend. This is where the real power has come from.

A high five to Alice for typing up my manuscript. You have been such a blessing.

To a fellow author, John Regan and JV Self-Publishing for the publication of *3 Peas in the 70s*, heartfelt thanks.

Reconciliation is the greatest act of love; hopefully, this theme is woven into these pages, opening your eyes to see the beauty of the words penned in this sequel to *3 Peas in a Pram*.

Lastly, to the God who created all things.

May we, the sheep of your pasture, give you thanks forever.
May we show forth your praise to all generations.

Amen

Rosie Farrow, 2021

Appendix of Help and Support Groups

- National Health Service, Tees.
- Insight Healthcare Talking Therapies - Phone 0300 5550555
- Open Minds - Phone 01642 218361
- The Samaritans - call anytime day or night. Phone 116123
- Book by Max Lucado, entitled 'Anxious for Nothing' - Finding calm in a chaotic world
- <u>God is our help too!</u>

Go to him in prayer. Whether in your home, on a park bench, in your car, in prison, wherever, he is ready to hear your prayer. Simply trust as you come near to God, He will come near to you.

Psalm 18 states He reached down from on high and took hold of me.
He drew me out of deep waters. He rescued me from my powerful enemy,
from my foes, who were too strong for me.
They confronted me in the day of my disaster
but the Lord was my support.
He brought me out into a spacious place;
He rescued me because he delighted in me
GOD DELIGHTS IN YOU!

- Book by Fuchsia Pickett, entitled 'Stones of Remembrance.' - A short account from chapter three is as follows:

"Saturday morning, I went to my study with every bone in my body feeling as if it were breaking, especially in my spine. A pain hit the base of my neck, went down my spine, shot into both of my legs and seemed to jerk my backbone. I fell to the floor and cried in pain."

After being admitted to hospital, the doctor fitted her into a brace, and she was sent home. The following Sunday, after taking medication for the pain, Fuchsia attended a church service at the First Pentecostal Holiness Church in Danville, Virginia. She felt so ill, she was ready to meet her maker. At the end of the service, the Holy Spirit told her, "Go forward for prayer."

Dragging her weakened body to the preacher, he prayed and anointed her with oil. After turning to go back to her seat, the power of God struck the base of her neck and coursed through her body.

She records, "The miraculous, healing power of God, put me back together instantly...I had been struck by resurrection power, which healed and set me free.

Within a few days of my healing, I realised that the baptism of the Holy Spirit I had received that day had ushered me into a new relationship with God."

Like myself, Fuchsia desires for this generation to know what has happened in her lifetime after being touched by God's supernatural power and revelation.

Printed in Great Britain
by Amazon

70497608R00088